AF574768

BALLROOM DANCING

By

MAURICE JAY

MAGNA PRINT BOOKS
LITTON, YORKSHIRE

First Published in large print 1975
by
Magna Print Books
Litton, Skipton, Yorkshire
by arrangement with
W. & G. Foyle Limited
London

© Large Print Edition 1975
Magna Print Books

ISBN 0 86009 030 2

Printed in Great Britain

CONTENTS

PART I — INTRODUCTION

PART II — THE DANCES

PART ONE
INTRODUCTION

[1]

DANCING AS A SOCIAL ASSET

IT surely cannot be disputed that of all the accomplishments man acquires to fit himself for the social scene, the ability to Ballroom dance is the one most universally favoured.

Desirable as it is to be a good bridge or tennis player, or excel at any other of the many social pursuits that occupy our leisure time, the opportunity to dance occurs more frequently than any other pastime.

It has the advantage of being enjoyed by every age and every class. It is indeed class-less.

Ballroom dancing is a common pursuit that bridges the gap between nations and races, and, although enjoyed more amongst the Western peoples, it is becoming accepted as a social practice by virtually every nation in the world.

It is a great social equalizer. When kings and

queens meet, a ball is held. When royalty meet the people on social occasions, it is often in the Ballroom.

When on the ballroom floor, it is one's ability to dance smoothly to the music and rhythm, and not appearance alone, that matters.

Bad dancers on a ballroom floor stick out like a 'sore thumb'—and are just as uncomfortable to themselves and their fellow dancers!

Our own Royal family are well aware of this fact, since they were taught to dance properly at a very early age.

Yet cuiously enough, there is still a certain strata of society, and in particular certain branches of the Armed Forces, which clings to an out-moded belief that it is 'not done' to dance well! Like the old saying that being a good snooker player is evidence of a mis-spent youth!

Yet surely if a thing is worth doing, it is worth doing well?

In this age of crowded roads, no one is allowed to take a vehicle on the road without some prior knowledge of the behaviour expected of him. Until he does possess that knowledge he proclaims to the whole world that he is a learner!

A dancer who has not mastered the elementary 'Rules of the Ballroom' is like a rogue elephant, dangerous to all who go near him!

Yet there *are* rules of the Ballroom as well as rules of the road, as you will see in a later chapter.

A Brief History of Ballroom Dancing

Dancing was one of man's earliest manifestations of his striving towards civilization. It may be that the original idea came from animals, birds and insects, who used it as a form of communication. Music and Rhythm too were copied from the sounds of birds and animal life, and from the rhythms of nature.

But when we talk of Ballroom dancing we refer to the dancing that is performed and enjoyed within man's domains and in places where people assembled. As far as this country is concerned it is safe to assume that Ballroom dancing proper began with the coming of the first Elizabethan Age. Shakespeare makes many references to the Court Balls and the somewhat robust nature of the dancing that took place. It was even said that the Earl of Leicester went too far and hoisted Queen Elizabeth I up by the buttocks, but it is recorded that the Queen evidently enjoyed this!

Those who decry the present trend of Rock and Roll take note!

Very soon however, dancing became solemn and formalized, with much stately parading, bowing and curtseying, as befitted a pastime enjoyed by the Queen and her Courtiers.

Louis XVI went further and commanded that all his Court, and in particular his commissioned officers, should learn to dance, 'thereby befitting themselves to be more proficient in the arts of war!' Nowadays that is done more on the barrack square than in a dance studio.

But these illustrations do show that dancing was taken very seriously and had become an accepted social grace. Queen Elizabeth I appointed official teachers of dancing (dancing masters they were called) and anyone who practised the teaching of dancing without a Royal Warrant was liable to the death penalty! Things are easier today, fortunately, but it is still wiser to go to a qualified teacher of dancing who is a member of a Society of Dance Teachers recognized by the ruling body, the Official Board of Ballroom Dancing.

So Ballroom dancing continued through the centuries with constant improvements and changes in dances and in rhythm up to the beginning of the twentieth century.

The coming of the First World War altered

many things and broke down many barriers. One of the first things to change was the age-old customs and behaviour in the ballrooms. At the same time new rhythms and new sounds were reaching England from other parts of the world—in particular the New World.

The Coming of Syncopated Music

As dawn broke on the twentieth century, the influence of the rapidly increasing negro population in America brought an awareness of their own distinctive kind of music and rhythm.

From the area around New Orleans came the first of the coloured musicians, playing music that had its origins in the jungles of their native Africa. At first it was called syncopation, which simply meant that the length of timing given to each note of music was broken up, according to the interpretation given to it by the musician.

Musicians used to improvise and give their own interpretation to a tune, and always there was this solid insistent beat behind it all, a relic of those far-off days when the jungle tom-toms were the only means of communication over distances.

So began the *Jazz Age.*

Just prior to the First World War, this gay,

uninhibited music reached England, together with another strange, rather exotic rhythm from South America—the *Tango.* Originally performed as a rather exotic folk dance by the Gauchos, or cowboys, of Argentina, it had been tamed into a ballroom dance of rather intense steps and compelling rhythm. 'Tango Teas' became all the rage, and a new social development, the *Thé Dansant,* the 'Tea Dance', became the thing.

Another new social innovation, informal dancing in the afternoon, also became accepted. However, Ballroom dancing up till then was very much the pastime of the upper and middle classes. Balls and assemblies, as the more popular dance gatherings were called, were very formal and dignified affairs, with set programmes, dance cards and introductions to your partner.

It was the carnage in Europe and the serviceman's search for relief from the horrors of war that finally completely changed the scene in the Ballroom. Coupled with the new uninhibited Jazz music, social and class barriers broke down as the wildly gay soldiers improvised new steps and danced with complete abandon during their all-too-short periods of leave from the battlefronts.

'Rag-time' they called this new dancing.

Obeying no rules, they just gaily 'danced' walking movements to the exciting new dance tunes. Gone was the sedate atmosphere of the pre-war balls and dances. Informality, both in dancing and in conduct, became the key-note. It was a feverishly-exciting period that finally put an end to rigid discipline that had previously governed the dances of the period.

From all this great upheaval was born modern Ballroom dancing as we know it today.

Until then, the bulk of the dances that made up a dance programme were either the set, sequence dances, like the Quadrilles and the Lancers, or the Waltz. It is interesting and amusing to note that, sedate and dignified as the Waltz was regarded, even in Victorian days, when it first appeared on the Continent around 1820, it swept through the stately homes of Europe like wildfire. So much so, that the reigning Pope thundered against this immoral new dance, which allowed a gentleman to so forget himself as to put his arm around a lady's waist and hold her close!

But even the Waltz, under the influence of the new exciting music of the early 1920s, lost a little of its dignity and instead of its gentle rotary movements, became more progressive in its action, and so more in accord with the new natural technique.

Dancers, dancing in couples and fitting their steps to music as they pleased, instead of following a set pattern or set routine, did away with the old technique of precise body and foot movements. With no one to guide them, no rules to follow and no patterns to remember, dancers began to make up their own steps and to be more natural in their body and walking actions. From these undisciplined beginnings came the foundations of the technique of modern Ballroom dancing.

It will be seen, therefore, that modern Ballroom dancing is based on natural walking and running actions. A step that was counted slow began to be taken on the heel, whilst the quicker steps were taken on the toe.

The feverish gaiety of the post—1914—18 period continued to be reflected in the ballrooms and café society, culminating in that wildest of all dances—the *Charleston,* with its high-kicking movements becoming a menace to those trying to dance a little more sedately.

Yet out of this chaos, orderly and standardized steps were to emerge.

The Coming of Modern Dancing

A small group of teachers operating in the West End of London, got together and formed a committee, out of which developed the standard four dances that form the basis of our dance curriculum today.

Under the chairmanship of the Grand Old Man of Dancing, Philip J. S. Richardson, O.B.E., this committee, which included Victor Sylvester, set to work and produced a technique of steps for the *Waltz, Quickstep, Tango* and *Foxtrot, The Standard Four,* as they are known wherever the *English Style* is danced today.

With subsequent modifications and additions, the technique laid down by this small band of dance teachers in the middle twenties is adhered to at the present time.

They took the dances, steps and rhythms as they found them and applied their own experience and a good deal of common sense to form what are basically quite simple movements in keeping with the character of the dances concerned.

How each of *The Standard Four* developed its own individual characteristics makes interesting reading.

Development of the Waltz

The Waltz, nowadays referred to as the 'Old-fashioned Waltz', had held sway in ballrooms for nearly a century. It was based on the Ballet technique, with its five foot positions, and danced on the toes. It was known as the Rotary Waltz, since it consisted of right and left turns danced with a full turn, so that the direction of the dance continued in a straight line down the room and was danced at a fast tempo.

The *Modern* or *Diagonal Waltz* as it was first called, took on an entirely new appearance. The tempo slowed down to nearly half the original tempo and only three-quarters of a turn was used for each turning figure. Thus instead of dancing in a straight line down the room, the figures took on a diagonal direction, first to the right and then to the left. The new technique of commencing figures by stepping forward on to the heel was also applied to the Waltz, and rising to the toes was done gradually over each set of three steps.

So the Waltz became a smooth, slow, but lilting dance in which the basic pattern created is that of a triangle instead of a circle. Since the end of the last war, the Waltz has taken on a more dynamic and colourful characteristic, but the basic pattern remains the same.

The Waltz is the easiest dance to learn because of the simple musical pattern of three beats to the bar, each of equal duration. Since most Waltz figures are made up of sets of three steps, a beginner is enabled to follow the music easily, as each step takes one beat of music.

Origins of the Quickstep

After the wild cavortings that at first accompanied 'Rag-time' music had died down, the earliest and most elementary form of dancing to this new syncopated music was known as the 'One-step'. This consisted, as its name suggests, of a simple walking movement, each step being taken to a 'slow' count of music, straight down the room and turning the corners by the simple process of closing the feet and moving off down the next 'line of dance'.

Towards the end of the First World War, a new dance called the *Foxtrot* reached this country from America. Originally a stage dance, its characteristic little walking and running movements were ideally suited to the new 'Jazz' music. Thus the now familiar *Slow Slow Quick Quick Slow* music pattern became the characteristic rhythm of the wildly-successful Foxtrot. The music for this dance was played at a slower speed than the 'One-step', and for the first time in modern dancing, the 'Chassé' was used, a 'Chassé' being a simple step-close-step movement, ideally suited to turning steps and figures.

This soon became adapted to the faster moving 'One-step' and the result was that the 'Foxtrot' as it was now called, was the name given to any dance, with widely varying tempos, that was danced to *Jazz* music.

Soon, however, our expert dancers began to evolve a more smoothly flowing and slower dance which did not include the 'chassé' type of step for turning movements. The faster type of dancing, which still used the 'chassé', became quite popular owing to its adaptability to any tempo. This latter dance became known by the cumbersome title of 'Quick-time Foxtrot' whilst the Foxtrot became the 'Slow Foxtrot'. In time these simple became known respectively as the *Quickstep* and the *Foxtrot,* and are so named today.

The Quickstep, with its faster tempo and its characteristic walk and chassé, is much easier to learn than its more sophisticated relative the Foxtrot, and for that reason is always taught before the Foxtrot.

The Quickstep is undoubtedly the most popular dance today, yet there are still dance band leaders who will persist in calling all 4/4 or rhythmic musical numbers Foxtrots, regardless of their tempo.

The Foxtrot Today

The Foxtrot, or the Slow Foxtrot, as it used to be called, is unquestionably the classic of the four standard dances. Its development owes much to the keen dancers of the 'Twenties, who, in an endeavour to lend more grace and smoothness to dancing, became fascinated by the rhythmic style produced from the long gliding steps that characterize the Foxtrot today. In aiming to perfect these long, smooth steps, they found that their movements were helped by discarding the 'chassé' type of turn, that is, the closing of the feet before moving forward, and substituting an 'open' type of turn, in which the feet passed one another instead of closing. Today, all the basic turns in the Foxtrot are 'open turns' as distinct from 'chassé' or 'closed' turns.

There is no doubt that the great improvement in the standard of Ballroom dancing, Contrary Body Movement, Sway, Rise and Fall, etc. (all of which are dealt with in later chapters), are the result of the study of the Foxtrot by the early pioneers. They soon began to appreciate the tremendous dynamic power of the body when in movement, from which discovery has resulted the lovely controlled dance that constitutes the Foxtrot today.

Newcomers to Ballroom dancing, having mastered the basic steps of the Waltz and Quickstep and then progressed to the Foxtrot, soon appreciate that more than mere knowledge of the various figures is needed to master the smooth flow of the Foxtrot. One reason for this is that nearly all the basic movements of the Waltz and Quickstep are of the type where one foot closes to another, with the next movement being started on the opposite foot.

In the Foxtrot one movement glides into the next almost imperceptibly as the result of one foot *passing* another, instead of closing to it; at the same time the body is continuously on the move. It is this that the beginner finds hard to achieve at first, and is consequently advised to master the Waltz and Quickstep first.

How the Tango became an English Ballroom Dance

The Tango started life as a rather crude

peasant dance enjoyed by the patrons of the less reputable cafés in the Argentine seaports. It arrived in this country via Paris where it had been performed largely as a stage exhibition number. By 1920 it was the thing for café society to patronize the 'Tango Teas' that were being held in many West End hotels, but the dance then bore little resemblance to the Tango that is danced today.

It was not until it became accepted as a competition dance, that our leading dancers, with their flair for movement, streamlined it and made it peculiarly English. Even today, you will find the Tango danced on the Continent with a good deal more Latin fervour and more dramatic steps than in this country, although our style is accepted by all nations in competitions.

Originally the Tango was danced to the 'habanera' type of rhythm, with a musical timing of two beats in the bar, that is: 2/4 time. An example of this rhythm can be found in that lovely old tune *La Paloma.* The modern Tango, however, in keeping its more streamlined appearance, is danced to a 'milonga' rhythm. Although written in 2/4 time, this sounds more like a Foxtrot rhythm, although the accented beats, characteristic of the Tango, are still maintained by the rhythm section of a dance band.

The Tango is not a hard dance to learn, certainly not as hard as the Foxtrot, yet many dancers are loath to take the floor when Tango music is played. Once again I cannot help feeling that this is because there are still a good many misconceptions about the Tango, mainly held by older people whose conception of the Tango was derived from seeing Rudolph Valentino perform it in some of his epics. The sad fact is that the Great Lover would look rather stupid doing the same dance on an English ballroom floor today!

No, the Tango is as English today as the Waltz, and our standards of performance are the envy of every country where the English style is taught.

To sum up, then, it will be seen that none of these four standard dances have been invented, as it were, but have been taken from original dances and rhythms from various countries. The Waltz from the Continent, the Foxtrot from America, and the Tango from the Argentine. The Quickstep we devised from the Foxtrot.

With that facility the English possess for adopting and adapting any new idea that captures their imagination, we have taken modern Ballroom dancing and raised it to a level that is the envy of all Western nations.

[2]

THE RULES OF THE BALLROOM

BALLROOM dancing, like any other activity, has certain fundamental laws governing its conduct which have to be followed wherever people are congregated in a limited area, all wishing to interpret individually whatever dance or rhythm is being played.

The first rule to learn is that of direction. Dancers move around a ballroom floor in an *Anti-Clockwise Direction.* Without going into the reasons for this, you will find that it makes for easier progression round the floor. If you do not understand why, try going round the floor in a *clockwise* direction and you will soon find out!

It must also be remembered that in modern dancing, although all the basic figures are standardized, there is no compulsion to use them in a set order. It will be seen therefore, that even though a dance floor can be crowded with dancers, by knowing in exactly which direction a step is started and finished, it is easier to keep the flow of dancing going. This enables individual couples to dance different figures without crashing into one another!

It is very important therefore, when learning to dance, to pay great attention to the direction of a figure. The term we use for this is *alignment.* It is to be remembered that very few figures in modern Ballroom dancing are executed with a complete turn, that is, finishing a step in exactly the same direction in which you started it. You will find this fully explained in Chapter 10.

Most basic figures are danced with *three-quarters of a turn.* Either to the right or to the left. Thus if you commence a right-hand figure, you will start by facing the outside wall in a diagonal direction and will finish it facing the *centre* in a diagonal direction.

It is also important to remember that no figure should be used which will take you in a backward direction for many steps, since you will be dancing against the flow of the rest of the dancers, or to use the correct term, *against the line of dance,* and that would be like driving a car in a busy English street on the right-hand side of the road!

Although over the years many varied and sometimes complicated steps have been devised, you will find that the basic steps contained in this book follow the directional rules that I have explained already. These basic steps form the complete background to all the four dances and are the foundations on which all other steps are built.

One last thing on the rules of the Ballroom. You will find that the words *Natural* or *Reverse* are used to describe the turns, or to preface the name of a figure.

We use the word 'Natural' when we mean to the *right* and the word 'Reverse' when we refer to the *left*. To any readers with inquiring minds who may wonder why this is so, the explanation is that owing to the fact that we dance in an anti-clockwise direction, it seems easier, or more natural, to turn to the right than to the left. The word 'Reverse' is therefore used in the sense that it is the reverse or opposite to natural.

I remember an amusing story concerning this fact. A very earnest and aspiring student was given an opportunity to take a class of small children. In endeavouring to instil into their young minds why they turned to the right and the left, he must have confused them, because the mother of one girl rang me up to ask what this 'Un-natural' turn was that her daughter had been taught!

[3]

NATURAL BODY ACTION AND MOVEMENT

I FEEL that it is essential before going on to explain the natural walking and running actions used in the Ballroom, to clear up the many widely held misconceptions about modern Ballroom dancing that still exist.

It must be remembered that modern Ballroom dancing has been created within the living memory of those who can recall the early Twenties of this century.

It is those people who could dance before the start of the First World War who are firmly convinced that modern Ballroom dancing is simply their style of dancing brought up to date.

Nothing could be further from the truth.

Old-time dancing, as it is now called, to distinguish it from modern Ballroom dancing, was the stylized, formal and rather artificial, posing attitudes that had originated in the time of Louis XIV of France and continued, with modifications, up to 1914.

It was based primarily on the ballet, with its five foot positions and its posed body postures. The delicate stepping forward, with the toe meeting the floor first, is quite contradictory to the natural action of modern Ballroom dancing where we dance, as we walk, with the heel meeting the ground first. Yet most people, if asked the question, 'which part of the foot touches the ground first when you walk along or take a step?' would reply, quite instinctively, that the toe meets the ground first. Well, try it for yourself. Simply look down when you are walking and see what happens to the feet! Then try to walk by touching the ground first with your toe and see how artificial it is.

So we have made our first point and cleared up the most popular error concerning modern Ballroom dancing; we dance as we walk, but with a good deal of conscious control necessary for a smooth, timed step.

Here then is a simple but thorough description of what happens to the feet and body when dancing.

The Use of the Body when Dancing

When the layman thinks of dancing, he automatically associates it with the legs and the feet. In actual fact, the first thing that one discovers when learning to dance properly is the supreme importance of the body.

If one thinks about this it will become obvious that this is so.

In commencing any step or movement it is the body that moves first!

If the body is turned to the right or left, or is taken forward, the legs and feet must *move with it.*

But it does not *follow that if the legs move forward, the* body *will automatically follow them!*

Try the following exercise and see for yourself whether this is so:

Stand perfectly upright with the legs straight and the feet close together. Without moving transfer your weight to the left foot (call this the supporting foot). Keeping the body perfectly upright, but without stiffening the body or legs, let the body incline forward until the weight of it is felt over the balls of the feet. Still maintaining the weight on the left foot, continue to incline the body forward. You will find that the forward pull of the body will take the right foot with it, and literally *compel* it to move forward!

In this simple lesson, one discovers a basic dynamic fact about the use of the body when dancing.

Even the Lady, whose role is to follow and therefore will feel that her steps are mainly backward (although this is not so, as I shall explain later), must be sure that her weight is slightly *forward* all the time; otherwise, if she stepped back and took all her weight with her, she would immediately fall on to the backward moving foot, with the result that she would pull the man forward with her and cause him to lose balance control.

If you would like to conjure up a mental picture of a couple dancing, think of the letter *K*, as in this sketch:

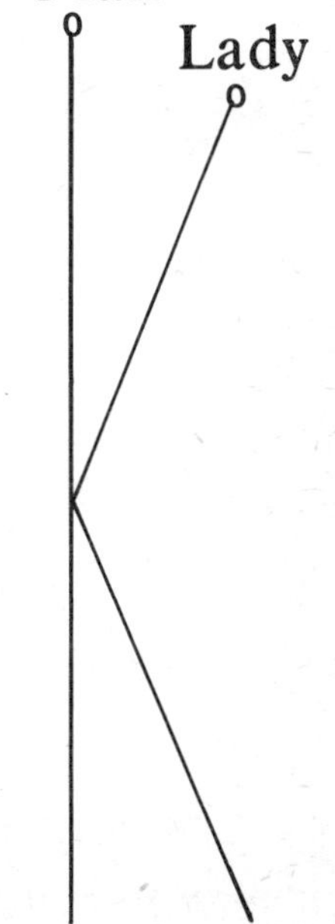

The controlled use of the body is also necessary to enable the Man to execute turning steps, as well as a means of controlling his own and his partner's balance, whilst the more advanced and 'dramatic' step simply could not be executed without the bold use of the body.

How the body is used, is explained in the following chapter.

[4]

THE USE OF CONTRARY BODY MOVEMENT

CONTRARY Body Movement (or C.B.M. for short) is the action of the body in relation to the moving foot. Here then is a description of Contrary Body Movement:

Place your feet together, body upright and inclined forward so that the weight of the body is felt over the balls of the feet.

Take the weight on to the left foot and prepare to take a natural length stride forward with the right foot, at the same time commence to turn the *left hip and shoulder* towards the moving foot.

Make sure that the right foot keeps in line with the left foot as it moves forward and you will know that you are using Contrary Body Movement when you feel your legs 'lock' at the thighs.

The application of C.B.M. to a step results in two important factors necessary to retain control over a step.

Firstly, it ensures that however bold and long a step is, you have maintained the correct balance of the body over the feet, by taking the *opposite* half of the body with you. Try this for yourself and at the fullest extent of your stride, see that your left shoulder is felt over the right heel.

The second factor is that using C.B.M. and feeling the legs 'lock' at the thighs, ensures that both legs are in line with one another. This prevents the moving leg going off at a tangent to the body, a common fault with most learners and poor dancers.

Read the above paragraphs in conjunction with the chapter on 'The Walk', which shows what happens to the feet and legs when taking a step; then try practising the walk, using C.B.M. at the same time, and you will soon feel the sense of balance and control over any walking step.

Remember that this action is used both by the Lady and the Man when *moving forward.* The exact opposite applies when moving backward. If the left foot is moved backward, the right hip and shoulder turn towards it. This is a little more difficult to master owing to the necessity, particularly for the Man, for keeping the weight forward whilst moving backward.

It is important for a lady to master the feeling

of C.B.M. when moving backward since the first, or leading, steps of any figure or turn are commenced by the Lady moving backward.

The Importance of C.B.M. when Turning

The use of C.B.M. is also of great value in assisting turning steps. Not only does it make it easier for the body to swing into a turn, but from the Man's point of view *it gives a clear indication to his partner that he is going to turn,* particularly if it is remembered that the *body initiates all turns.*

It will be seen therefore, that the correct application of C.B.M. is of great value for four reasons:

1. It enables a walking step to be taken with greater control and balance.
2. It helps a dancer to keep his feet in line with each other on all straight steps.
3. It assists all turning movements.
4. It gives a clear indication, through the body, that the Man is preparing to turn.

It is well worth the time spent in practising walking movements using C.B.M., since it makes a would-be dancer continuously conscious of the part that the body plays in dancing.

Fig. 1. Contrary Body Movement Position

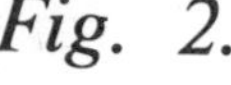

Fig. 2.

Fig. 3.

Fig. 2. The wrong way
See how the Man has allowed his partner to be left on his right side. The left hand has dropped down and the body tilted over in his attempts to maintain balance. Although a step of this kind (a Lockstep) should be danced on the toes, see how the Man has made no attempt to do so.

Fig. 3. The right way
See how close contact is still maintained at the hips although the Man is dancing the figure outside his partner. Notice the correct and upright hold and stance, with the Man well up on his toes.

Contrary Body Movement Position [C.B.M.P.]

Having discussed the importance of the use of C.B.M., we cannot leave the subject without referring to Contrary Body Movement Position (C.B.M.T.). See Fig. 1.

This is the action of taking one leg well across or behind the body, when dancing an outside step. The reason for this is to prevent loss of contact at the hips when a man dances a step outside his partner.

There are quite a number of figures where the Man, instead of stepping in line with his partner, takes a step 'outside', or to her right side. If the Man merely stepped straight forward he would lose contact with his partner and a rather ugly body line would be created.

Figs.2 and 3 are illustrations demonstrating the right and wrong way to dance a step with the partner outside.

Notice how the Man has broken his elegant upright stance as shown in the correct illustration. In the illustration showing an 'outside figure' being badly danced, the unfortunate girl's head has almost disappeared under his right arm, due to the fact that instead of the Man keeping contact with his partner, he has just danced on in his own sweet way, leaving his partner to catch him up as best she could!

You will find that Contrary Body Movement Positions occur in many steps in all dances, whenever the Man is stepping outside his partner, or the Lady is brought forward outside the Man. Loss of contact at the hips not only creates bad body lines, but also results in the Man losing his control over his partner. Contrary Body Movement Position (C.B.M.P.) is therefore important if an elegant stance is to be maintained whatever figure is being danced.

When we come to discuss the Walk (*see* chapter 6) it is important to remember that whilst this chapter concerns the action of the legs and feet, the application of C.B.M. to any walking or leading steps has always to be borne in mind.

[5]

LEADING AND FOLLOWING

ONE of the most important aspects of modern Ballroom dancing is for the Man to acquire a good strong lead so that the Lady is always made aware of what he is about to do. This is because there are no set figures or sequences to follow.

Once a man knows a sufficient number of figures to make his dancing varied and interesting, he can please himself in what order he uses them, although it is important to know what appropriate steps to use at any given position.

He alone, therefore, must be in charge, as it were!

The Lady must never anticipate or try to lead him into a figure. Remember, ladies, at all times the Man is the boss!

At the same time, the Lady can be a great help in assisting the Man by keeping good hip contact and knowing her own steps well! That is why the Hold and the position of the arms are so important.

The Man, whatever figure he is dancing, should at all times endeavour to maintain his arm and shoulder line.

How then, should the Man indicate to his partner what he is going to do?

This is done through the turning action of the body (C.B.M.) and the firm pressure exercised through the wrists and hands, without distorting his appearance.

The Lady, on the other hand, can help her partner tremendously by being firmly balanced, keeping her hips well towards her partner and by never leading forward, so that he has to push his partner out of the way before he can progress!

A dancing partnership, to be enjoyed, depends on the Man's ability to know his steps well enough to ensure that he can give a thought to leading his partner into figures without treading on her toes through lack of indication. But however well the Man can dance, if the Lady is not prepared to follow him, or is quite oblivious of what he is doing, then the dance will not be enjoyable.

Many an anticipated happy evening has been spoilt because the Man has not made dancing a pleasure, through his poor performance. At the same time, many a man's enjoyment has been ruined and his illusions shattered by a sweet face and slim figure that seemed to weigh half a ton as soon as they stepped on to the dance floor!

Leading and following are two of the successful ingredients that go to make for happy dancing.

A last thought for the Man. It is not only what you can *do* on the dance floor that makes you a good dancer. It is also *what you can make your* partner *follow!*

[6]

THE WALK

ONE of the first things a human being learns to do at a very early stage in life is to walk. That is to say, he becomes conscious that it is his legs and feet that will enable him to reach any given object in front of him.

When we talk of the Walk in Ballroom dancing, we do not mean the instinctive action of walking, but the controlled placing and stretching of the leg and foot to enable us to take a measured length stride in time to music, at the same time adjusting our step to our partner so that at all times we appear to be gliding effortlessly around the ballroom floor.

It is necessary therefore to analyse thoroughly what happens to the legs and feet when dancing. In a previous chapter I mentioned that most people have never given a thought to what actually happens when they take a step, and very often think that a step is taken with the toe meeting the ground first.

It therefore must be emphasized that the Walk, as used in modern Ballroom dancing, is simply the natural action of a walking step, taken deliberately, with due regard to everything that happens *in* a walking step. The first thing that occurs in the training of a soldier, actor or actress, mannequin or model, is that *they are taught to talk!* In Ballroom dancing, the Walk is of paramount importance. When the Walk is thoroughly understood and mastered, you are half-way to becoming a dancer.

Practice in the Walk, therefore, is essential if your wish to dance well and at the same time, *look* a dancer!

The Forward Walk

Commence feet together, weight over the balls of the feet.

Fig. 4. The Walk, showing dancers at the fullest extent of their stride. Notice the bold forward sweep of the body, and the way in which weight is exactly distributed between each foot. The Man's weight is supported by the heel of the front foot and the ball of the back foot, whilst the Lady's weight rests between the heel of her front foot and the ball of her back foot. Note the firm contact by both Man and Lady at the diaphragm, with hips well forward.

By remembering to use a slight C.B.M. action you will find this will greatly assist your balance. Remember, too, that in taking a stride, it should be a perfectly natural movement. The leg swings quite freely from the hip, almost in a pendulum action. There is no artificial forcing of the leg or any part of the leg.

Remembering these points, commence by taking the weight on to the left foot and allow the right foot to move forward.

As it moves forward, the ball of the foot should be in contact with the ground. This will happen quite naturally if the supporting leg (that is, the left foot) is kept slightly flexed, acting as it were, as a spring or shock-absorber.

As the right foot continues on its journey, the whole of the foot should be felt skimming along the floor.

As the stride continues, with the leg moving quite freely from the hips, the toe of the moving foot will naturally leave the ground, with the result that the remainder of the stride will be continued with the heel skimming the floor.

At the same time as the moving heel passes the supporting (L) toe, the left heel will be released from the ground (*see* Fig.4).

At the fullest extent of the stride you should be

equally balanced between the heel of the front foot and the ball of the back foot.

Try practising this walking action and see if you can hold the position perfectly poised so that you could rock back or forward on either foot, without losing your balance.

To Continue the Walk

Remember that the body is still being carried through with the leg, and at the fullest extent of the stride, *both legs are straight, but not stiff.* Now transfer your weight to the front foot and allow the toe to lower to the floor (the body will push the foot down if you let it, anyway). At the same time commence to draw your back foot forward, but endeavour to retain a little weight on the back foot. (The idea of trying to retain a little weight on the back foot as it is drawn forward is to produce a gliding movement as well as being able to keep control of the feet at all times.)

As the back foot continues to be drawn forward allow the knee of the front foot to relax a little, to enable the back foot to be kept skimming the floor. This is one of the hardest things to acquire, but having done so, you will begin to feel that you are acquiring control over your leg muscles which is so essential for a smooth balanced stride.

Continue to bring the back foot forward until the feet are parallel and continue with the left foot in another walking action.

Having mastered the continuous gliding movement from one step to another, try a series of continuous steps around the room.

When you feel that you are getting the controlled, smooth, feel necessary, try taking the steps to music. Any slow rhythmic tune will do, the slower the better at first. Count 'slow' as you do so, i.e., two steps to a bar of music.

Points to Remember

Always aim to use each part of the foot in turn, from the toe to the heel and the heel to the toe. Feel that each part of both feet touches the floor in turn: the heel, the whole foot, the ball of the foot and the toe.

Remember that the feet never leave the floor entirely, there is always *some* part of both feet in contact with the floor (except in the Tango).

At the fullest extent of the stride, the legs are straight but not stiff.

Think of the knee supporting your weight as a shock absorber, which gently gives as the weight of the body passes over it.

Always practise it in conjunction with a slight Contrary Body Movement (*see* Section [4]).

Start with small steps first and increase them as you become more balanced and controlled.

The Backward Walk

Whilst it is essential for the Man to master the Backward Walk, the Lady, in particular, since moving backward is her dominant role, must be able to step back and at the same time give support to her partner, by controlling her steps through the legs and feet.

While this description of the Backward Walk is for both Man and Lady, it must be remembered that the Lady wears high heels when dancing (not too high, I hope!) and will appear to let her heel come to rest on the floor immediately she steps back.

The legs of the Lady, therefore, should always be well braced to receive the weight of the body as it moves over the supporting foot, and not try to keep her heel off the floor, because of the height of her shoe heels.

Description:

Commence with feet together, knees relaxed,

and the weight of the body felt slightly over the balls of the feet.

Begin to take a natural length stride, swinging from the hips, as in the Forward Walk, going first on to the ball of the foot, then the toe, then the ball of the foot again, at the same time releasing the front toe.

At the fullest extent of the stride the body should be centrally poised over the heel of the front foot and the toe of the back foot (*see* Fig.4).

The legs should be straight (but not stiff) at this point.

The next part is the most difficult and should be thoroughly understood. Commence to draw the front foot back with slight pressure on the heel (*see* notes on Forward Walk) *taking care not to lower the back heel until the moving foot draws parallel.*

The reason for this is that if the heel is lowered immediately the back foot is in position, the body will fall backward too quickly and result in a bumpy and lurching action, so destroying the smooth controlled flow that all dancers aim for.

It is essential that the weight is kept slightly forward or difficulty will be experienced in lowering the heel of the supporting foot at the right time, that is, when the feet come together.

Again, when practising this movement, the use of slight Contrary Body Movement assists in maintaining control and balance. Practise this moving around the room as in the Forward Walk until you can feel that the smooth transference of weight from one foot to the other, whilst the feet are passing, can be accomplished without falling back on to the back foot before the stride is completed.

Points to Remember

As the moving foot swings back, do not allow the front foot to move until the toe is naturally released from the floor. If your weight distribution is correct, you will feel the slight pressure on the heel of the front foot as it commences to move back.

Do not allow the weight of the body to push the supporting heel to the floor immediately the stride backward has been made. Remember that it gradually lowers as the front foot is drawn towards it.

It has been said that 'If you can walk, you can dance'. This is certainly true. But only when the 'walk' is done as has been described above.

Learn to 'walk' smoothly, in a controlled manner, and you have gone a long way to becoming a dancer.

[7]

RISE AND FALL

IF Ballroom Dancing were to consist merely of steps danced to music and given a certain musical time value, it would be lifeless indeed.

What gives Ballroom dancing its character and depth of feeling is the use of the body, legs and feet by rising and lowering according to the steps being danced.

We call this 'Rise and Fall'.

In the Quickstep and the Foxtrot there are slow steps and quick steps. In most slow steps we dance as we walk, commencing by stepping forward on to the heel. The quick steps we dance on the toes.

In the Waltz, so as to give it its characteristic lilting action, we commence by taking the first step down, leading with the heel, and rising to the toes during the second and third steps.

There are exceptions to this general rule, but there is always a reason for them.

The Tango has no Rise and Fall, as will be

explained later.

What must be appreciated, however, is that Rise and Fall in dancing is not merely the action of rising to the toes and then lowering again. It is felt throughout the body, starting from the toes, and every part of the body, from the feet, through the ankles, legs, hips, to the diaphragm (but *not* the shoulders), is utilized. It is a feeling of pressing up from the floor, of breathing in and bracing the body upwards, that creates Rise and Fall, which should be thought of as a mental action, rather than as merely a physical reflex. It developes as an upward surge of the body rather than as an automatic rising to the toes, coupled with a strong body lead, as the result of having used C.B.M. together with quickening of the step, as in the Quickstep and Foxtrot. This process creates Rise and Fall.

It is essential therefore that the mechanics and principles of the walk are fully understood, particularly the part that the knees play in creating soft movements.

Let me explain.

Rising to the toes as used in dancing is, in effect, rather like a mild form of jumping or vaulting action. If, for instance, you wished to vault over a fence, or jump over a hurdle, what would you do? You would first of all flex your knees, to create a tension that is released as the legs straighten and you jump.

That is precisely what happens in Rise and Fall.

The knee softens, just prior to rising to the toes, and creates a tension, as in a spring, that enables you to rise, through the body, and thus create an effortless-looking movement that gives so much expression to Ballroom dancing.

It is also important to see that your poise is correct. By this I mean that the weight of the body is felt over the balls of the feet, so that your body is not thrown backward by the rising action of the legs and body.

Rise and Fall varies with each dance. In the Waltz it is stronger and deeper than the Foxtrot and Quickstep. There is no quickening of steps in the Waltz as there is in the Quickstep and Foxtrot. Each step has a beat to itself. Therefore the knee relaxes more in the Waltz to give the necessary tension to rise to the toes at the end of the first step. The rise, too, is more gradual than in the Foxtrot. It commences at the end of the first step and continues through the second and third steps and then lowering at the end of the third step.

In the Foxtrot, owing to its more progressive nature, the rise is more abrupt. It is felt at the end of the first step of a movement, which is usually a slow step, and is held for the following two quick steps that usually follow, lowering at the end of the third step.

In the Quickstep, the faster speed of the dance makes the rise much easier, just as it is easier to jump when running than when walking.

The knees, in addition to helping the rise, also help to govern the speed of rising and falling. For example, the knee action will be slower in the Waltz than say, the Quickstep, for obvious reasons.

In the Waltz section (*see* Part II Section [1]) you will find some simple exercises in which Rise and Fall can be practised.

The Rise and Fall of any step must not be so abrupt that it can be seen to happen.

It must be hidden in the flow of the dancing.

The knees must not flex until the weight of the body is over them. In this way the knees can control the speed of the Rise and Fall.

[8]

THE USES OF SWAY

ALTHOUGH the learner will find Sway hard to feel or execute at an early stage, there is no doubt that a knowledge of the principles governing it will considerably assist the execution of turns and other figures, once the steps themselves have been mastered.

What is Sway?

It is the slight inclination of the body from the feet upwards and is used to assist turning movements as well as give an artistic effect to other figures. The use of sway gives an added refinement to the execution of figures, and whilst a learner will not be bothered with it at first, one can never become a good dancer without understanding its use and putting it into effect.

Broadly speaking, Sway is simply the application of a fundamental dynamic force to Ballroom dancing, and is born out of the correct use of C.B.M. and Rise and Fall.

The principles that govern Sway are also those that govern any other moving object. For, example, when you turn a corner whilst driving a car or riding a bicycle, what happens? If you turn to the right, you will find yourself swaying or leaning to the right. If you turn left the body will incline to the left.

You are simply obeying a natural dynamic law.

So it is with dancing.

Here is an example of the application of Sway in the Waltz.

Natural Turn (First three steps)

Forward *right* foot turning body to the right. Body straight. 1.

Left foot to the side, still turning. Body sways to the right. 2.

Turning on ball of left foot, close right foot to left foot. Body holds sway to the right. 3.

Note.—C.B.M. is used on Step 1 *as it is a turning movement.*

This general principle is followed on all basic figures, with a few exceptions.

Generally speaking, the rule followed is that if a turn is commenced on the *right foot,* the following two steps will be taken with Sway to the *right.*

If a left or reverse figure is used then the body

will sway to the left following a leading or commencing step taken with the left foot.

There are exceptions to this rule, but where they occur, an explanation will be given.

In more advanced figures, Sway is also used for effect, but a good standard of dancing should be achieved before this type of figure is used.

[9]

FOOTWORK AND FOOT POSITIONS

Footwork

The term 'Footwork' is applied to that part of the foot in contact with the floor at the time of stepping, and its subsequent positioning. It must always be remembered that every step has a start and a finish, so the footwork does not remain the same throughout the step.

This chapter will indeed repay careful study, since attention to footwork will result in much neater foot action, and will show what an important part the ankles have to play.

There are six Footwork positions, (*see* Fig.5) which will be referred to later when the various dance figures are described in detail:

They are as follows:

1. Heel.
2. Toe.
3. Ball of foot.
4. Whole foot.
5. Inside edge of foot.
6. Inside edge of toe.

Generally speaking, only the terms Heel and Toe are used, but it is sometimes necessary to refer to the other parts of the foot. For example, the starting or leading step of any figure will always be taken on the heel when moving forward and is normally counted slow.

A step taken back is usually given with the footwork 'Toe, then Heel'.

Most slow steps are taken on the heel, and most quick steps are taken on the toe.

In the Waltz the first step is taken on the heel and the second and third step on the toe, with a few exceptions.

In the Tango, owing to its individual characteristics, some steps are taken on the inside edge of the foot.

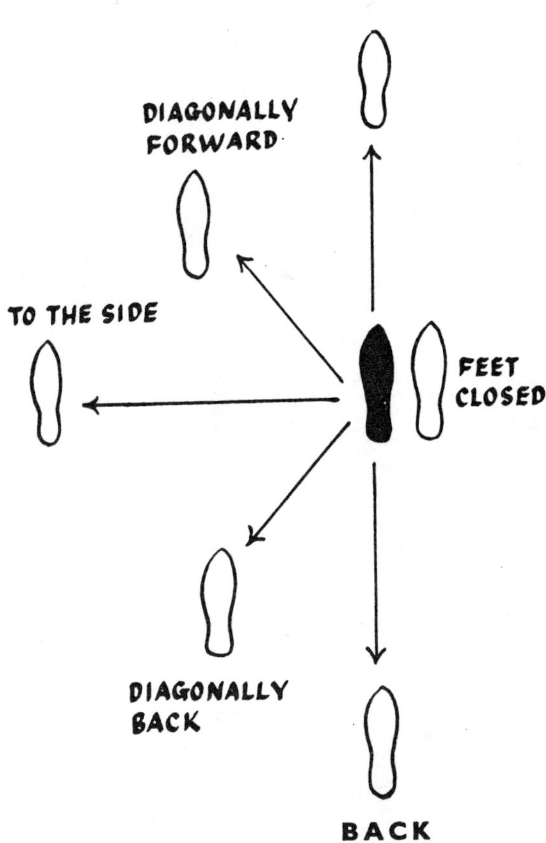

Fig. 5. Foot positions
The six foot positions generally used in the description of steps are shown in this diagram. Two other foot positions are sometimes used: 1. To the side and slightly forward. 2. To the side and slightly back. These will be explained when used.

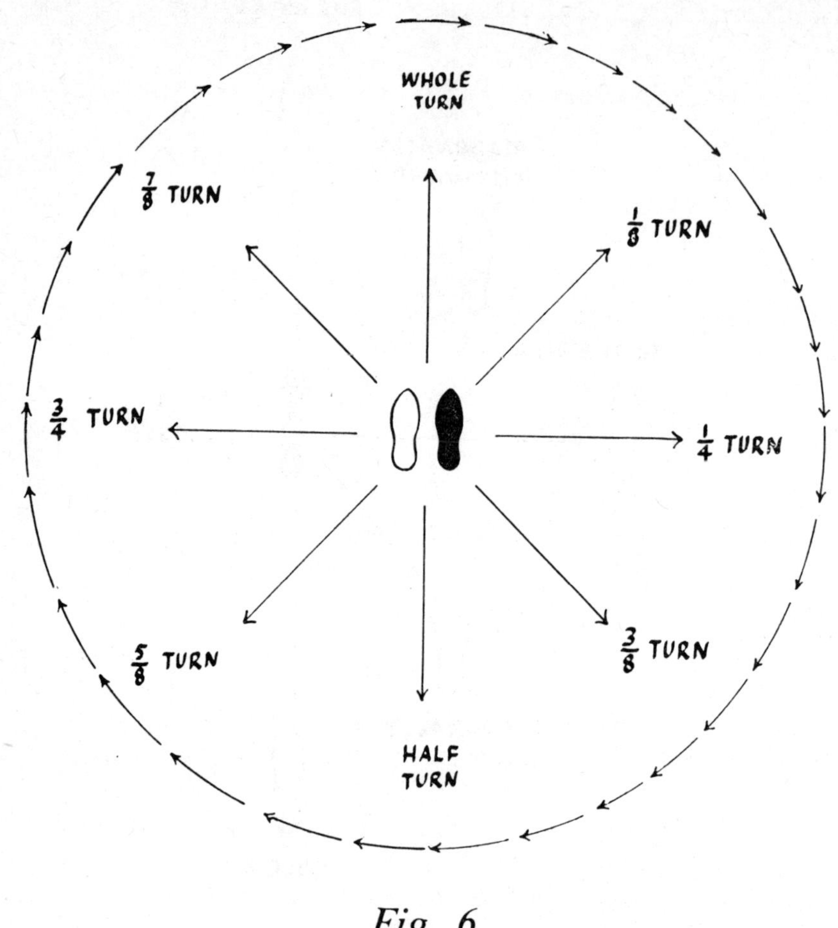

Fig. 6.

[10]

THE AMOUNTS OF TURN USED

FOR the purpose of calculating how much turn is used in a figure, the best method is to position yourself in the centre of the room and imagine yourself as the centre of a circle; then mentally divide the circle into eight equal parts.

If you follow the diagram and turn to the right a segment at a time, you are turning an eighth of a turn each time.

When you arrive at your original alignment you have completed a full turn. (*see* Fig.6.)

When working out an amount of turn given in the descriptions of steps, the following is useful to remember:

If you face up the room preparing to dance in an anti-clockwise direction around it, the table below will give you the amounts of turn, together with the alignment.

Turning an eighth of a turn to the right.
(Diag. = Diagonally, L.O.D. =Line of Dance)

Amt. of Turn	*Alignment*
1/8	Facing diag. to wall
1/4	Facing wall
3/8	Facing diag. wall against the L.O.D.
1/2	Facing against L.O.D. (or backing Line of Dance)
5/8	Facing diag. centre against L.O.D.
3/4	Facing centre
7/8	Facing diag. centre
Whole Turn	Facing Line of Dance.

These terms are also used (as in the case of the Lady and some men's steps) prefaced by 'Backing' instead of 'Facing'.

The amounts of turn for every figure are given with the description, but it is often very useful to practise the amounts of turn as given in the diagram and associate each amount of turn with its equivalent alignment. The exact amount of turn used in each step is not so important as remembering the amount of turn used over the whole figure, or, as in the case of the basic steps, each part of the figure.

In the case of the Natural and Reverse turns in the Waltz, Quickstep, Foxtrot and Tango, the starting and finishing positions, as well as the amount of turn used, are exactly the same for all three dances.

In the Natural Turns of all dances, they are normally commenced facing diag. to wall and finished diag. to centre, but can be started facing Line of Dance.

The Reverse Turns are commenced diag. to centre or facing L.O.D. and finished diag. to wall. If you consult Fig.6 you will see that the amount of turn used is three-quarters.

When you come to the descriptions of the various figures, you will notice that the fourth step of every turn is always taken back down the Line of Dance as Man, and forward down the Line of Dance as Lady. This is a generally observed rule but has a few exceptions.

Thus it will be seen that all the turns are so contrived that whilst they commence either diagonally to the wall or to the centre, the 1st step of the second half of a turn is taken down the Line of Dance, and it is this that preserves the flow of people dancing different figures yet all proceeding in a uniform direction.

A dancer with a good sense of alignment seldom bumps into anyone and a thorough understanding of the amounts of turn used in the various steps is a great aid to achieving this sense.

Dancing a Turn as a Couple

The observant reader, when studying the descriptions of the Basic Turns, may notice that the instructions for turning are not the same for the backward part of a turn as they are for the forward part of a turn.

When dancing the first three steps of say, a Natural Turn, the description is:

1. Forward right foot, turning body to the right.
2. Side left foot, *still turning.*
3. *Still turning on left foot,* close right foot to left foot.

Notice therefore, that the last three steps, the backward part of a Basic Turn, are as follows:

4. Back left foot, turning body to right.
5. Side right foot, across Line of Dance, *still turning right, pointing toe down Line of Dance.*
6. Close right foot to left foot (notice, no 'still turning').

If you study the two descriptions closely, you will notice that on the *first* three steps *the turn is spread over each step.* On the last three, the 2nd step is already in position on step 2 and there is no further foot turn, although the body has still to complete the turn, since the Man or Lady dancing the forward part of the turn completes his or her turn on the 3rd step.

The reason is that on the forward part of a turn the person is dancing on the *outside* of a turn and therefore covering more ground than the person on the *inside.* It is therefore easy for the person on the outside of a turn to spread the turn over the three steps. On the other hand, the person on the inside of a turn finds the turn much more compact, the 2nd step going into its finishing position whilst the body completes the turn on the 3rd step.

A simple example of this fact is to watch a record spinning on the turntable. The label, which only occupies a small area in the centre of the record, obviously covers less ground in its revolutions than the outside grooves of the record itself, but the label, being stuck on, keeps the same relationship to the record all the time.

A dancing couple, being two separate moving bodies, are not so fixed and the differences in the amounts of turn danced at the same time are as explained above.

[11]

THE TERMS USED IN DANCING

MUCH of this book so far has been devoted to explaining the various factors and aspects of modern Ballroom dancing which will help the layman to obtain a good understanding of what makes the whole thing 'tick', as it were.

I have done this for two reasons.

One is that it should lead to a quicker and better understanding of figures to be described later in detail.

The other is that if the reader appreciates the general principles already discussed and applies them wherever possible to the various figures, much unnecessary brain-searching can be avoided when studying the step-by-step descriptions.

If, for instance, it is thoroughly understood that Contrary Body Movement is used on all turns or parts of turns that initiate a movement, this can be automatically applied as a matter of principle, rather than having to remember the C.B.M. for each individual step. Where there are exceptions to these fundamental rules, they will, of course, be explained, with the reasons for them.

In the list that follows, an explanation is given of the various terms which will be encountered in Part II, where the dances and figures are described in detail. They will well repay a thorough study.

TECHNICAL TERMS

A Turn

Although the word 'turn' is normally used in its generic sense, it is specifically used to mean the type of turn used in the Basic Turns, that is, the Natural and Reverse Turns in all dances. It is the gradual turning action over the two separate sets of three steps that usually makes up a Basic Turn.

Most Basic Turns are made up of six steps in two sets of threes. The first three is the Man's forward part and the Lady's backward part, and the last three is the Man's backward part and the Lady's forward part.

A Pivot [Man]

A Pivot is the type of turn which is made *on one foot only,* and can be used to the left or to the right. Pivots are normally danced after 1, 2 and 3 of a Natural or Reverse Turn, and are therefore commenced when the Man has his back to the Line of Dance and is preparing to step backward.

Here is a description of a Pivot as used in the Natural Pivot and Spin Turn.

Commence feet together, backing the Line of Dance. Feet flat.

Take a small step back with the left foot, at the same time taking a strong turn to the right with the body (*see* C.B.M.).

When the weight of the body is felt on the ball of the back foot, pivot half a turn to the right, at the same time keeping the front foot (R.F.) in front of the body with thighs locked (C.B.M.P.).

Remember that although moving backward it is important to keep the weight of the body slightly forward.

When the Pivot is completed, your position will be that you are now facing down the Line of Dance with the weight still on the ball of the back foot, with right foot extended in front of you.

This is an action best practised solo, since the Lady's step differs slightly. To practise the pivoting action return to your original position with the feet together and keep trying the pivoting action.

[Lady]

The Pivoting Action for the Lady is commenced by stepping forward and pivoting on the ball of the right foot, keeping her left foot behind her.

In the case of the Lady, however, she will not find it possible to keep her legs in the 'locked' position since the nature of the Natural Pivot will make her back leg move to the left slightly, although this must be controlled as much as possible.

Reverse Pivots

When dancing a Reverse Pivot, however, both Man and Lady will find it quite possible to keep their legs 'locked'. The only way to understand the reason for this is to try for yourselves, but one of the reasons is that in a normal hold in dancing the Lady is held slightly to the Man's right side and the tendency is for the leg of the Lady in a pivoting action to slip slightly more to his right. In a Reverse Pivot, owing to the nature of the movement, this tendency is corrected. For that reason we say that, in a Natural Pivot, the Lady dances a pivoting action, whilst the Man dances a true pivot.

A Spin

A Spin is another turning action in which the turn is made *on one foot only,* but the other foot, instead of being kept forward or back, is usually placed to the side of the spinning foot at the completion of the spin.

In the case of the Natural Pivot and Spin Turn (which is usually abbreviated the 'Spin Turn'), the turning action following the pivot is continued on the outstretched leg (right foot) and the body spins on the ball of the right foot with the left finishing to the side of the right foot and slightly back from it.

Toe Pivot

Although called a Toe Pivot, this is a misnomer, since the action is more akin to a spin, but in the case of a Toe Pivot, the weight is retained on the *spinning foot* and not transferred to the *closing foot.*

A figure using this type of spin is called the Double Reverse Spin. One of the advantages of a Toe Pivot is that it allows a whole turn to be danced in three steps, whereas in a basic type of turn, only three-quarters of a turn is danced over six steps.

A Heel Turn

This is, as its name suggests, a type of turn danced on the heels, and is used by the Lady when the Man is dancing a Foxtrot—or 'Open'—type of turn. It is in fact used on most steps when the Man needs a smooth continuous type of turn or spin.

The idea behind a Heel Turn is that the Lady, by turning on one heel and transferring her weight to the closing foot, covers a very small area and thus enables the Man to swing smoothly around her using an 'open' turn.

Heel Turns are essentially a Lady's step and should be practised diligently. What is more, however expert a male dancer is, he could never lead a Lady into a Heel Turn by indication alone. She must know how to do it herself. A Lady's Heel Turn, neatly done, plays a great part in helping her partner to lead her smoothly and neatly.

Here is a description of a Heel Turn to the right (Natural):

Step 1. Back left foot, turning body to right.

Step 2. Commence to turn on the *heel* of the left foot, at the same time draw the *heel* of the right foot to the left. About three-eighths of a turn is made between these two steps so that the Lady is facing the Line of Dance at the end of the 2nd step.

Step 3. Having completed the turn on the heel of the left foot, the weight is transferred to the heel of the right, and the left moves forward down the Line of Dance.

A Lady should practise this on her own so that she can transfer the weight from one heel to another without losing her balance.

To be able to dance a neat and balanced Heel Turn is the hallmark of a competent dancer and is well worth the practice spent on it.

It is also worth remembering that there are many popular figures that cannot be danced by a Lady unless she knows her Heel Turns.

A Hesitation Step

This is a movement where one foot is drawn or brushed to the side of the other and moves off in a forward or backward direction without the weight of the body being transferred to it. To make this clear, remember that it is usual to take one step at a time with alternate feet, so that as one foot closes to another, the weight is usually transferred to the closing foot. In this figure, it does not.

Although the term Hesitation might suggest

that the feet pause or hesitate, this does not really happen, but the movement slows up, giving an effect of a pause in the flow of the dance.

This step is used in the Waltz, in the Natural Hesitation Change, and its use here is a valuable one, since it allows a couple to swing immediately from a right turn to a left turn without any intervening 'linking' movements. To avoid any temptation to transfer the weight, the usual Rise and Fall of the Waltz is not felt, the feet being kept flat. In this way a Man can convey to his partner that he is not changing his weight.

A Heel Pull

This is the last half of a Man's Foxtrot Natural Turn, where one heel is drawn to the other whilst the turn is made on the supporting heel. It differs from a Heel Turn inasmuch as the Man brushes the moving foot forward, instead of transferring his weight as in a Lady's Heel Turn.

The Heel Pull is not an easy step to master, but is invaluable in learning the foot control so necessary if the Foxtrot is to be enjoyed.

Outside Partner

The term 'Outside Partner' occurs often in the descriptions that follow, and simply means that the Man steps outside his partner, instead of in line with her feet. Care must be taken in using a step taken outside one's partner, since it is so easy to lose contact at the hips, with the result that an ugly body line will be created.

As mentioned elsewhere, whenever a step is taken outside partner, Contrary Body Movement Position must be used. That is to say, the moving leg must be taken across the body to prevent loss of contact with partner.

Partner Outside.

This position is created by the Man bringing his partner back outside on to his right side and the same precautions must be taken as in Outside Partner.

Steps and their Time Values

Slow. A slow step is counted as two beats in a bar of four beats in 4/4 time, as in the Quickstep and the Foxtrot. In 2/4 time, as in the Tango, a slow step takes one beat, or half a bar.

Quick. A step counted quick will take one beat in 4/4 time and half a beat in 2/4 time. Thus the number of steps that can be danced in a bar of music are as follows:

2 slows to 1 bar
1 slow and two quicks to 1 bar
4 quicks to 1 bar

Note.—In Waltz music all beats are of equal duration, one step per beat, three beats in the bar. In some Waltz steps, however, what are known as 'syncopated' beats are used. Four steps are danced to a bar of music and to do this one beat is 'split' or syncopated, usually the middle beat. The count for this is referred to as '2 *and*'. In a figure using four steps the counting will normally be '1, 2 *and* 3'. It is, in effect the same count as slow, quick, quick, slow in the rhythmic dances.

Tempo

This refers to the speed at which a dance tune is played and is calculated by the numbers of bars played in a minute.

For example, a Quickstep should be played at speeds varying from 48 to 52 bars per minute.

The Foxtrot 31 to 33 bars per minute.

The Tango 32 bars per minute.

The Waltz 30 to 32 bars per minute.

Dance tunes played above or below these speeds make it difficult to dance these dances correctly or with sufficient feeling.

Open Position

The term 'Open' is used in a number of different ways and the reader can be confused unless the distinctions are explained. Here are three of the ways in which the term is used:

Open Turn, as distinct from Closed Turn. This is to indicate that the feet are 'open' or passed, to distinguish the figure from a 'Closed' Turn where the feet are closed—or brought together—on the 3rd step.

Open Promenade. This means that the Lady is held at an angle from the hips of the Man, the couple being opened out fan-wise, as it were, as distinct from the normal in-line position, with the hips in contact.

The word 'open' can also be applied to a step in which C.B.M. is *not* used, that is to say, the legs are 'open' rather than 'locked' as when C.B.M. is used.

Abbreviations Used

L.	*Left*	Fwd.	*Forward*
R.	*Right*	Diag.	*Diagonally*
L.F.	*Left foot*	L.O.D.	*Line of Dance*
R.F.	*Right foot*	C.B.M.	*Contrary Body Movement*
S.	*Slow*	C.B.M.P.	*Contrary Body Movement Position*
Q.	*Quick*		

The Construction of a Dance

A dance is composed of:

Steps. That is, one single step.

Figures. Made up of a number of steps.

Variation. A figure which is not a basic figure.

Amalgamation. A number of figures, from two or more, linked together.

(*Suggested amalgamations are given at the end of the descriptive section for each dance.*)

PART TWO
THE DANCES

[1]

THE WALTZ

Introduction — Waltz Square — Turning Waltz Square — Closed Changes — Natural Turn — Reverse Turn — Natural Pivot and Spin Turn — Natural Hesitation Change — Reverse Corté — Whisk and Chassé — Drag Hesitation to Back Lock — Back Whisk — Double Reverse Spin — Amalgamations

Introduction

Waltz music being written in 3/4 time — that is three beats in the bar — most figures used in the Waltz are in sets of threes. Each step, therefore, has its own beat. The first beat of the bar is always heavily accented and the dance must always be started on the first beat so as to keep in time with the music.

Unless the Waltz is danced in time to the

Fig. 7. The Man's Hold
Note the upright, yet slightly relaxed stance, with knees also relaxed. The arms are nicely balanced, with the Lady's hand taken between the Man's thumb and fingers. The Man's left hand should be held sufficiently up to hold the Lady's arm level (as shown in the diagram) and his left forearm and Lady's forearm should come together to form an inverted 'V'. The head is turned slightly to the left. Feet and hips should be neatly in line with partner. Note the elegant, relaxed placing of the Lady's fingers along the Man's upper arm.

Fig. 8. The Lady's Hold

The hips are well forward to partner, and arms well balanced. The body is held slightly back from the Man above the hips. The head is turned to the left and held slightly back. Note the position of the Man's right hand, gently curved and passed under the Lady's shoulder blade.

REMEMBER:

The Lady's left hand should never be placed on *the shoulder, but just below it.*

The Man's hand and arm should be placed as shown, but should not be too tight. Any pressure or indication needed is expressed through the wrist only, thus keeping the rest of the arm in position. The Man's left hand should be at approximately ear level.

music it becomes meaningless, and when learning to dance it is better to wait and listen carefully to the accentuated first beat before starting.

There is another aspect of dancing which has not been mentioned before and which particularly applies to the Waltz. I call it 'musical phrasing', and even in the early stages it helps a beginner to appreciate the rhythm and swing of the Waltz.

To explain: Nearly all tunes composed or adapted for modern Waltz music use the chorus of a song only, seldom the verse. These choruses are invariably 32 bars in length and consists of the main musical theme (8 bars), the same theme repeated (8 bars), the 'middle eight' (8 bars) in which the tune goes off into a different theme, and then to finish, the original theme with an ascending musical ending (8 bars).

It will be seen that the tune is broken down into four sets of 8-bar phrases. If you listen to a modern Waltz tune being played, try to spot the way it is broken down; it is quite easy to follow.

Thus, when practising steps, if you miss the start of the tune, wait until you recognize the beginning of an 8-bar phrase and start then. It is surprising how the Waltz can be enjoyed more when you are not only dancing to its rhythm, but also its 'phrasing'. Try it!

Waltz Square

Although the Waltz Square is simply a practice routine, all that is basic in the Waltz is contained in this simple exercise, since it teaches you the basic pattern of the Waltz steps both forward and backward, and can be learnt and practised by both Lady and Man.

You will notice that the pattern made over the six steps forms a square (*see* Figs.9a and 9b) and should come quite easily after a few practices.

If you have never danced before, you may find a tendency to attempt to step back on step 4 with the same foot. Remember: one foot, one step, at a time!

After you feel that you can dance the Waltz Square without looking at your feet (always a habit at the start), try to dance it keeping the head up and looking straight forward. Now try it to music, remembering to wait for the accented beat and the start of a 'phrase'.

Points to remember:

Step *straight* forward or back. Do not let the foot go off at an angle to the body. When you step to the side on steps 2 and 5, make sure that the feet are parallel. Close with the toes together.

Rise and Fall:

Having mastered the actual steps and danced

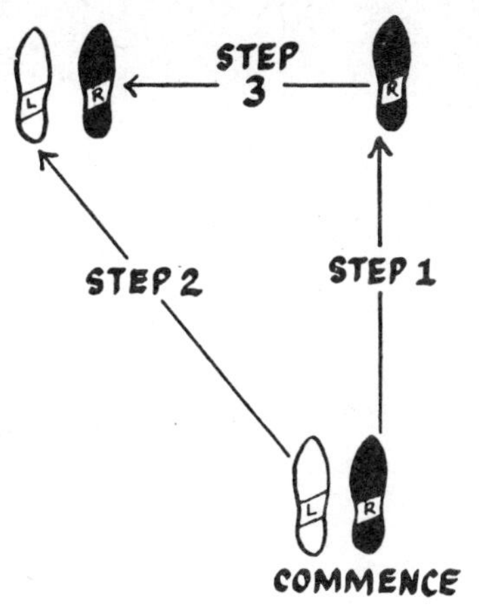

Fig. 9a.

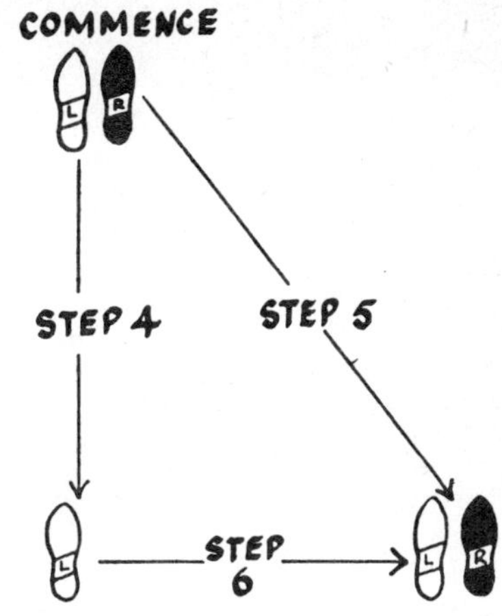

Fig. 9b.

Fig. 9a. Waltz Square—Forward
Starting position:
Feet together, weight on L.F.

Step No.		Beat No.
1	*Forward R.F.*	*1*
2	*Side L.F.*	*2*
3	*Close R.F. to L.F.*	*3*

Fig. 9b. Waltz Square—Backward
Starting position:
Feet together, weight on R.F.

Step No.		Beat No.
4	*Back L.F.*	*1*
5	*Side R.F.*	*2*
6	*Close L.F. to R.F.*	*3*

them to music, try the following:

Step 1. Step fwd. R.F. on to the heel, relaxing the knee slightly and prepare to rise to the toes.

Step 2. Step to the side on the toe of the L.F. and feel that you are still rising.

Step 3. Close R.F. to L.F., rising high on the toes.

Step 4. Step back L.F. at the same time lowering your right heel until the heel touches the floor. Feel the body start to rise at the end of this step.

Step 5. Step to the side on the toe of the R.F. and continue rising.

Step 6. Close L.F. to R.F. rising to the full extent.

Important!

Always remember to lower the supporting heel as step 4 is taken, and again when stepping forward after dancing the full six steps. Remember also that the rise is not sudden, but is started at the end of step 1 and continued through each step until the close at the end of step 3.

When lowering at the commencement of each movement (after the feet have closed high on the toes, that is) do so gradually, so that the lowering of the feet and body is hidden in the movement of the legs.

Practising the Waltz Square and using Rise and Fall will prove invaluable when you come to the figures of the Waltz, since the Rise and Fall will apply to most figures described.

Turning Waltz Square

We have now danced the Waltz Square to music, using Rise and Fall and the correct footwork. In the Turning Waltz Square, we learn the application of Contrary Body Movement, as well as starting to calculate the amounts of turn used. The Turning Waltz Square should not be attempted until the First Exercise is thoroughly mastered.

The Turning Waltz Square consists of twelve steps in four sets of threes. On each three steps you will be turning a quarter of a turn to the right, so that if your amount of turn is correct you will finish in exactly the same place as you started!

The best way to do this is to start facing up the long end of the room you are practising in. If you make a quarter of a turn over each three steps you will face a *different wall in turn at the end of every 3rd step,* bringing you back to your starting place at the end of the 12th step. This exercise, if

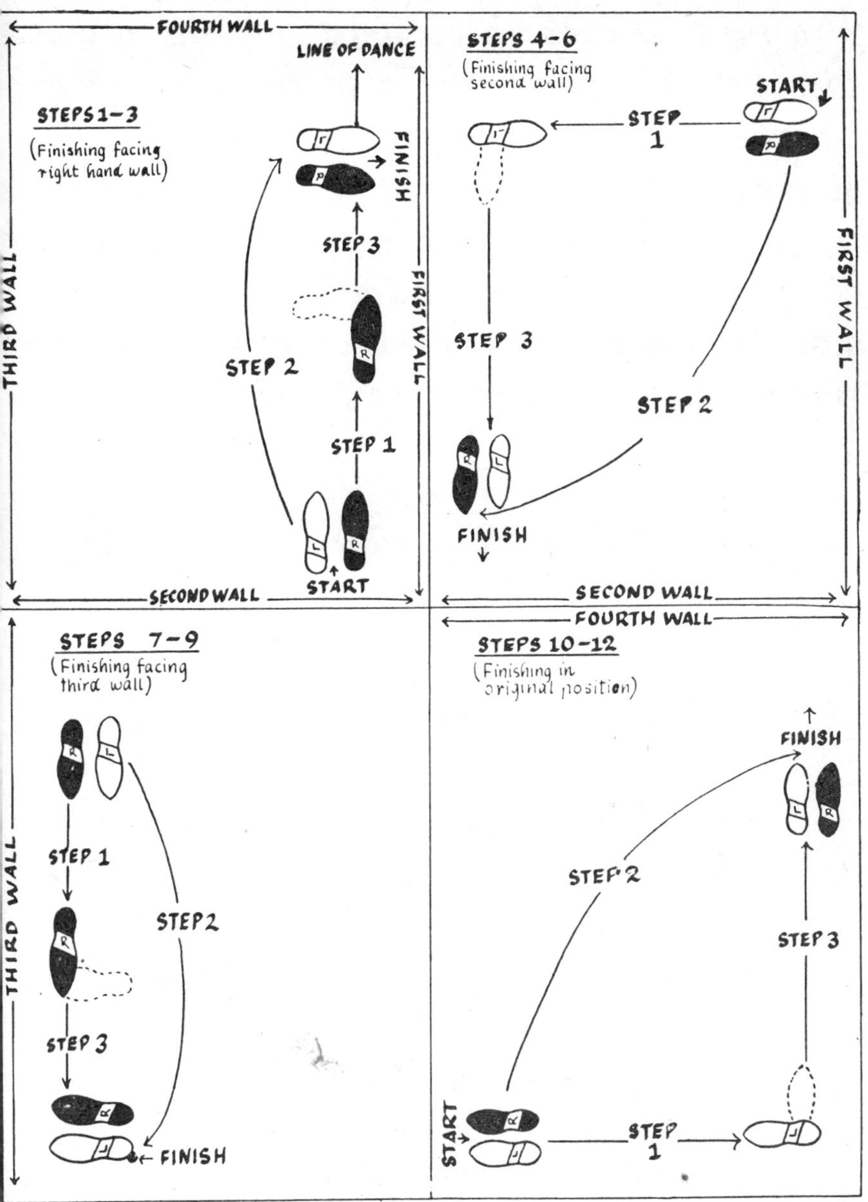

Fig. 10. Turning Waltz Square

Start by facing up the room. As you commence step 4, you will be facing the first wall. Commence step 7 facing the second wall. Commence step 10 facing third wall. You will thus dance a quarter of a turn on each three steps, making a whole turn over the twelve steps to finish where you started.

Important. *The dotted outline shown at an angle to steps 1, 4, 7 and 10 is* the position of the foot after the second steps have been taken to the side. *For the purpose of this exercise, all the foot turn is made between steps 1 and 2.*

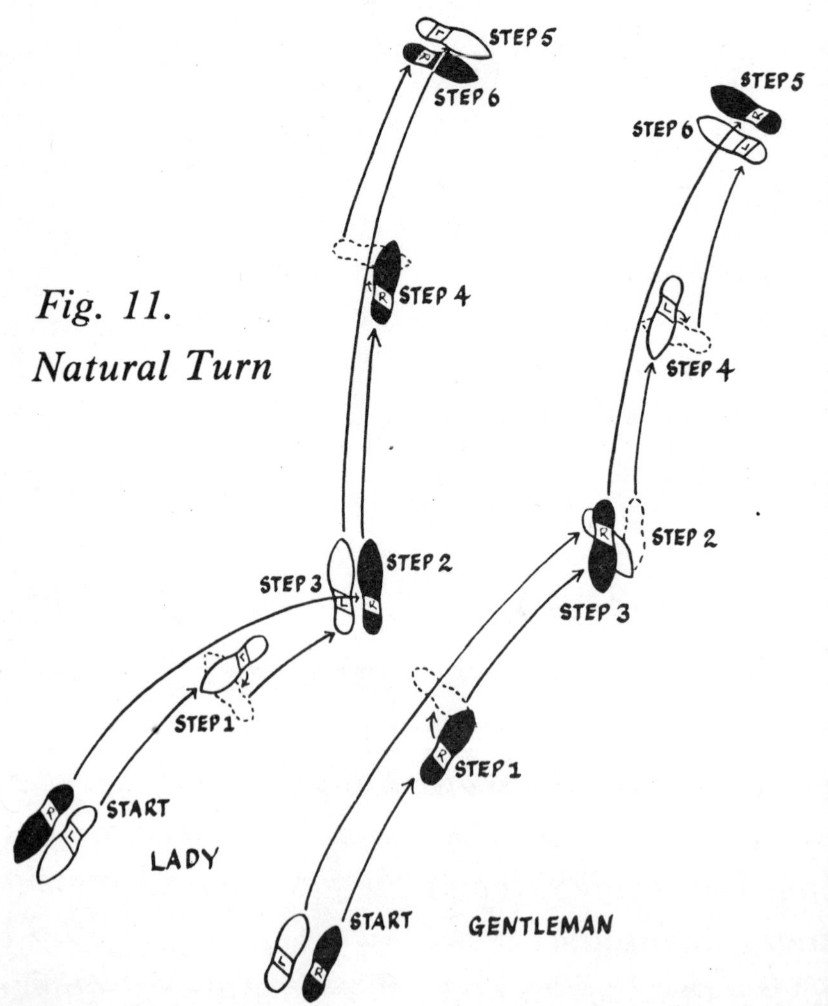

Fig. 11.
Natural Turn

thoroughly practised, will give you an insight into all the various factors that go to making a Ballroom dancer.

Closed Changes

The Closed Change Steps described here are exactly the same as those shown in the Waltz Square and are used in the Waltz to 'link' the figures together. They can, however, be used continuously, first R.F. start, then L.F. start, as a simple exercise which will help you to progress around the room.

MAN

Step No.		*Count*
1.	**Right foot forward. First heel, then toe.**	**1**
2.	**Left foot to side. Toe.**	**2**
3.	**Close right foot to left foot. Toe, then heel.**	**3**

LADY

Step No.		*Count*
1.	**Left foot back. First toe, then heel.**	**1**
2.	**Right foot to the side. On toe.**	**2**
3.	**Close left foot to right foot. First toe, then heel.**	**3**

Note.—If C.B.M. is used slightly, the Man will find his 2nd step moving slightly forward, and the Lady's 2nd step moving slightly back as well as to the side.

Continue now with the Closed Change, commencing this time with the Man's left foot and the Lady's right.

It will be interesting to note that with the slight use of C.B.M., a Closed Change taken on the right foot will turn you very slightly to the right, whilst a left foot Closed Change will turn you slightly to the left.

Remember, however, that if you feel confident enough to attempt to use C.B.M., do not let it deflect the 1st step from moving straight forward in line with the body. Such a deflection can produce a 'waddling' effect which looks ungainly.

It is important to master the figures described above before attempting any new steps.

Natural Turn

The Natural Turn is commenced when facing diag. to wall after a Change Step taken on the left foot. Three-quarters of a turn is made over the whole figure which will be finished facing diag. to centre.

This figure is, of course, the first turn that should be attempted after the Turning Waltz Square has been mastered.

It can also be used at a corner, when less turn will be used on the last three steps so that you are facing diag. to centre on the next line of dance.

MAN

Step No.		*Count*
1.	**Right foot forward diag. to wall, turning body to right. Heel, then toe.**	**1**
2.	**Left foot to side still turning to right. Toe.**	**2**
3.	**Close right foot to left foot still turning on L.F.—now backing line of dance. Toe, then heel.**	**3**
4.	**Left foot back turning body to right. Toe, then heel.**	**1**
5.	**Right foot to side still turning to right. Toe.**	**2**
6.	**Close left foot to right foot—now facing diag. to centre. Toe, then heel.**	**3**

LADY

Step No.		*Count*
1.	**Left foot back diag. to wall turning body to right. Toe, then heel.**	**1**
2.	**Right foot to side, still turning to right. Toe.**	**2**
3.	**Close left foot to right foot—now facing line of dance. Toe, then heel.**	**3**
4.	**Right foot forward turning body to right. Heel, then toe.**	**1**
5.	**Left foot to side still turning to right. Toe.**	**2**

6. **Close right foot to left foot still turning on L.F.—now backing diag. to centre. Toe, then heel.** **3**

General Note

Normal Rise and Fall, C.B.M. and Sway are used as explained in the chapters under these headings, and everything for the Lady is the normal opposite.

For the learner, this figure is usually followed by a right foot Closed Change into a Reverse figure.

Reverse Turn

This is exactly like the steps of the Natural Turn in every respect, except, of course, that it is commenced with the left foot, starting diag. to centre and turning to the left. In other words, it is the counterpart to the right-hand or Natural Turn, and by using these figures along the room alternately, linking up each turn with a Change step, a couple can progress around the room in an interesting and varied fashion.

MAN

Step No. *Count*

1. **Left foot forward diag. to centre, turning body to left. Heel, then toe.** **1**
2. **Right foot to side still turning to left. Toe.** **2**

3. **Close left foot to right foot still turning on R.F.—now backing line of dance. Toe, then heel.** **3**
4. **Right foot back, turning body to left. Toe, then heel.** **1**
5. **Left foot to side, still turning to left. Toe.** **2**
6. **Close right foot to left foot—now facing diag. to wall. Toe, then heel.** **3**

LADY

Step No. *Count*

1. **Right foot back diag. to centre, turning body to left. Toe, then heel.** **1**
2. **Left foot to side, still turning to left. Toe.** **2**
3. **Close right foot to left foot—now facing line of dance. Toe, then heel.** **3**
4. **Left foot forward, turning body to left. Heel, then toe.** **1**
5. **Right foot to side, still turning to left. Toe.** **2**
6. **Close left foot to right foot still turning on R.F.—now backing diag. to wall. Toe, then heel.** **3**

General Note

The Rise and Fall, C.B.M., Sway, amounts of turn are exactly the same as for the Natural Turn, since each turn is identical except for the difference in direction.

If this figure is finished near a corner, the next step taken forward will be in a direction diag. to wall on the left foot. This step could then become the 1st step of a Whisk (q.v.), and used to change direction along the next line of dance.

Spin Turn

This is an extremely useful figure for turning a corner, and as will be seen, consists of the first three steps of the Natural Turn, followed by a Pivot and Spin, making half a turn, and is ended with the last three steps of the Reverse Turn.

The amount of turn on the last three steps can be varied according to the next figure, and the turn can be finished either diag. to wall of next line of dance or facing *centre* diag. of new line of dance.

It will be found that if the Pivot and Spin are kept very compact it will be both easier to dance and easier for the Man to control and guide his partner.

MAN

Step No.	*Count*
1. Right foot forward into first three steps of Natural Turn—to finish backing the line of dance. (1) Heel, then toe. (2) Toe. (3) Toe, then heel.	**1,2,3**

4. Left foot back (medium length) turning body strongly to right, keeping right foot extended forward in front of left foot—now facing line of dance. Toe, then heel, then toe.	*pivot*	**1**
5. Extend right foot slightly forward, still turning to right. Heel, then toe.	*spin*	**2**
6. Continue turning body to right and step to side and slightly back with left foot—now backing diag. to centre. Toe, then heel.		**3**
7,8,9. Right foot back into last three steps of Reverse Turn to end facing diag. to wall (7) Toe, then heel, (8) Toe. (9) Toe, then heel.		**1,2,3**

LADY

Step No.	*Count*
1. Left foot back into first three steps of Natural Turn—finish facing line of dance. (1) Toe, then heel. (2) Toe. (3) Toe, then heel.	**1,2,3**
4. Right foot forward, turning body to right, keeping left foot to rear and to the left of right foot—now backing line of dance. Heel, then toe.	**1**

5. Transfer weight to left foot, still turning to right. Toe. **2**

6. Continue turning body to right, brush right foot to left foot, and step right foot diag. forward—now facing diag. to centre. Toe, then heel. **3**

7,8,9. Left foot forward into last three steps of Reverse Turn—now backing diag. to wall. (7) Heel, then toe. (8) Toe. (9) Toe, then heel. **1,2,3**

Notes for Lady

As will be seen from the description, after the Lady has commenced her pivoting action on step 4, keeping her left foot behind her, she will find that it tends to move to her left. Do not attempt to hold the leg rigidly behind but allow to move left quite naturally.

The 'brush' movement described on step 6, gives a neat finished look to the Spin, but no undue emphasis should be placed on it at first. It does, however, help to get the Lady's foot out of the Man's way as he completes his Spin.

General Notes

If the Spin Turn, taken at a corner, is finished facing diag. to wall on the next line of dance, the next step forward (left foot) can be made the 1st step of a Whisk, or a left-foot Closed Change into a Natural figure.

C.B.M., Sway, Rise and Fall, footwork, etc., are all normal for steps 1, 2 and 3, as well as 7, 8 and 9. To master the pivoting and spinning actions of steps 4, 5 and 6, see notes on the 'Pivot'. Care must be taken when pivoting on step 4 to avoid the temptation to rise. For both Lady and Man, the Pivot and Spin is made on the balls of the feet whilst keeping the feet flat.

On step 4 too, the Man must use strong C.B.M., at the same time keeping a firm pressure under the Lady's shoulder-blade with the heel of his right hand, so that she is fully aware of the nature of the step.

Both Lady and Man should practise this step solo before attempting it together, so that the nature of the movement is fully understood. Once mastered, the Spin Turn teaches the dancer much about the 'mechanics' of turns in dancing.

Natural Hesitation Change

The Natural Hesitation Change is an extremely useful figure in a crowded ballroom, since it enables a couple to swing from a Natural Turn into a Reverse Turn without having to use a

Closed Change step to 'link' them up.

Once the Man has mastered his own steps, he must use firm pressure with the base of his right hand on the Lady's back to indicate that her weight is held on the left foot (step 5). He must endeavour to keep the knee well relaxed on step 4 to avoid the instinct to rise. *Remember! There is no rise on steps* 4, 5 and 6 for either Man or Lady.

MAN

Step No.		*Count*
1,2,3.	**First three steps of Natural Turn —now backing line of dance. (1) Heel, then toe. (2) Toe. (3) Toe, then heel.**	**1,2,3**
4.	**Left foot back, turning body to right. Toe, then heel.**	**1**
5.	**Right foot to side of left foot, small step, still turning to right on heel of left foot—now facing diag. to centre. Heel, inside edge of foot, then whole foot.**	**2**
6.	**Hesitate, brushing left foot towards right foot, keeping weight on right foot, still facing diag. to centre. Inside edge of toe of left foot.**	**3**

Note: Continue into next figure by stepping forward left foot.

LADY

Step No.		*Count*
1,2,3.	**First three steps of Natural Turn— now facing line of dance. (1) Toe, then heel. (2) Toe. (3) Toe, then heel.**	**1,2,3**
4.	**Right foot forward, turning body to right. Heel, then toe.**	**1**
5.	**Left foot to side, still turning to right— now backing diag. to centre. Toe, then heel.**	**2**
6.	**Hesitate, brushing right foot to left foot, but keeping weight on left foot, still backing diag. to centre. Inside edge of toe of right foot.**	**3**

Note: Continue into next figure by stepping back right foot.

General Notes

Normal technique is observed on steps 1, 2 and 3, but there is no Rise and Fall on steps 4, 5 and 6. Slight Sway is felt on steps 4 and 5 and the body commences to turn to the left as the left foot brushes towards the right foot before moving forward (step 6) as Man. Lady normal opposite.

This figure is usually followed by the Reverse Turn or Reverse Corté.

Reverse Corté

Although a useful figure to have in one's repertoire, the Reverse Corté must be danced with care and consideration for other dancers, since it has a 'retrogressive' or slightly backward action.

It can be taken any time the left foot is free facing diag. centre, and is shown here with a simple ending.

This is another figure of the Hesitation type since the feet are closed on the 5th step (Man) and held for the 6th step. The Lady dances a forward, side, close movement.

Again, care should be taken by the Man to indicate the nature of the figure to the Lady by means of a strong right-hand lead.

MAN

Step No.		*Count*
1,2,3.	**First three steps of Reverse Turn—now backing line of dance. (1) Heel, then toe. (2) Toe. (3) Toe, then heel.**	1,2,3
4.	**Right foot back, turning body to left. Toe, then heel.**	1
5.	**Close left foot to right foot, turning body to left without changing weight—now facing diag. to wall. Heel, then toe.**	2
6.	**Hold position, weight still held on right**	

foot. Toes of both feet, then lower right heel. **3**

7. **Left foot back (diag. to centre against line of dance). Partner outside. Toe, then heel.** **1**
8. **Right foot to side, rather wide step. Toe.** **2**
9. **Close left foot to right foot, facing diag. to wall. Toe, then heel.** **3**

LADY

Step No.	*Count*
1,2,3. First three steps of Reverse Turn—now facing line of dance. (1) Toe, then heel. (2) Toe. (3) Toe, then heel.	**1,2,3**
4. Left foot forward, turning body to left. Heel, then toe.	**1**
5. Right foot to side, still turning to left. Toe.	**2**
6. Close left foot to right foot—now backing diag. to wall. Toe, then heel.	**3**
7. Right foot forward diag. to centre against line of dance, outside partner on partner's right side. Heel, then toe.	**1**
8. Left foot to side, medium step. Toe.	**2**
9. Close right foot to left foot, now backing diag. to wall. Toe, then heel.	**3**

Note for Lady

On step 7, when the Man brings his partner forward outside him, the Lady must endeavour to step forward with her right foot well across the body to avoid losing contact at the hips (C.B.M.P.).

General Notes

Normal technique is used on steps 1, 2 and 3, and 7, 8 and 9, but the rise is felt later on steps 5 and 6. Instead of finishing the movement with steps 7, 8 and 9, step 7 can be danced as the 1st step of a Back Whisk followed by a Chassé.

Whisk and Chassé

The Whisk and Chassé are really delightful figures to learn and are not at all difficult to master. This is the 1st step in the Waltz in which the Lady is turned to 'Promenade Position', that is, opened out fan-wise to form a 'v' between the two bodies.

Again, the importance of the Man's firm base-of-hand lead must be stressed, in turning the Lady to Promenade Position.

It is taken in a direction diag. to wall, and the following Chassé moves along the line of dance. Note the 'split' second beat of the Chassé, counted '2 *and*'.

MAN

Step No.		*Count*
1. **Left foot forward diag. to wall. Heel, then toe.**	*whisk*	**1**
2. **Right foot to side and slightly forward. Toe.**		**2**
3. **Cross left foot behind right foot in Promenade Position. Toe, then Heel.**		**3**
4. **Right foot forward in Promenade Position along the line of dance. Heel, then toe.**	*chassé*	**1**
5. **Left foot to side and slightly forward along the line of dance. Toe.**		**2**
6. **Close right foot to left foot. Toe.**		*and*
7. **Left foot to side and slightly forward. Toe, then heel.**		**3**
8. **Right foot forward diag. to wall, outside partner. Heel.**		**1**

LADY

Step No.		*Count*
1. **Right foot back diag. to wall. Toe, then heel.**	*whisk*	**1**
2. **Left foot diag. back commencing to turn body to right to Promenade Position. Toe.**		**2**

3. Cross right foot behind left foot in Promenade Position, now facing diag. to centre. Toe, then heel. *whisk* **3**

4. Left foot forward in Promenade Position down line of dance. Heel, then toe. **1**

5. Right foot to side, turning body to to left. Toe. **2**

6. Close left foot to right foot. Now backing diag. to wall, and square to partner. Toe. *chassé* *and*

7. Right foot to side and slightly back. Toe, then heel. **3**

8. Left foot back diag. to wall. Toe, then heel. **1**

Note for Lady

A charming and graceful effect can be achieved by the Lady in the Whisk if, as she crosses her right foot behind left (step 3) she turns her head very strongly to the left as if looking over her left shoulder. Care must be taken to see that the head is kept up and the eyes do not look down (a common fault, this).

The head can also be turned to the right as shown in Fig.12.

Note that the Lady's body turns 'square' to Man during steps 5 and 6.

General Notes

Remember that the Man does *not* turn to Promenade Position, but *turns his partner* to Promenade Position. He makes *no* turn but the Lady turns a quarter of a turn to the right during steps 1, 2 and 3, regaining her 'square to partner' position during steps 5 and 6.

Care should be also taken by the Man not to allow the Lady to turn too far out as an ugly body position will result and contact will be lost at the hips.

Normal technique is used in the Whisk with regard to Sway, C.B.M., Rise and Fall, etc.

Note that in the Chassé, a sustained Rise is danced as in the Progressive Chassé in the Quickstep.

The last step (8) is, of course, the first step of any Natural figure.

Make certain when preparing to dance this amalgamation, that you have enough room to finish it before reaching a corner or, if at a corner, dance the Whisk *into* the corner and then dance the following Chassé along the *next* line of dance.

Drag Hesitation and Back Lock

The Drag Hesitation and Back Lock is a

popular figure. One of its attractions is that it fits in smoothly along the line of dance, even though the Man is travelling backward. It usually follows a Double Reverse Spin finishing facing line of dance.

As its name implies it is a form of Hesitation movement followed by a Lockstep moving backward and can be ended either with a Back Whisk or, a simpler ending, 4, 5, 6 of a Natural Turn.

MAN

Step No.	*Drag Hesitation*		*Count*
1.	**Left foot forward down line of dance, turning body to left. Heel, then toe.**		1
2.	**Right foot to the side, on same line of dance. Toe.**		2
3.	**Still turning on ball of right foot, drag left foot to right foot,** *without weight.* **Toe, then lower.**		3
	Back Lock		
4.	**Back left foot, down line of dance, bringing partner outside. Toe, then heel.**		1
5.	**Back right foot, partner outside. Toe.**	*each half-beat*	2
6.	**Cross left foot in front of right foot. Toe.**		*and*
7.	**Back right foot, partner outside. Toe, then heel.**		3

Then back left foot, partner outside, into next figure.

Note for Man

As left foot closes to right foot in step 3, firm pressure with the base of the right hand on Lady's back will convey to her that she is not to change the weight. At the same time she is brought more to the Man's right side to allow her to be taken forward on his right side.

No Sway, and the Rise is a step later than usual (on step 2), lowering at the end of 3 and rising at the end of 4. Then up to the end of the figure.

LADY

Step No.	*Drag Hesitation*		*Count*
1.	**Right foot back down line of dance, turning body to left. Toe, then heel.**		**1**
2.	**Left foot to side on same line of dance. Toe.**		**2**
3.	**Drag right foot to left foot without putting weight on it. Toe, then heel.**		**3**
	Back Lock		
4.	**Right foot forward, outside partner. Heel, then toe.**		**1**
5.	**Left foot diag. forward. Toe.**	*each half-beat*	**2**
6.	**Cross right foot behind left foot. Toe.**		*and*

7. Left foot diag. forward. Toe, then heel. 3
Then forward right foot into next figure. Rise, Fall and Sway normal opposite to Man.

General Note

The Drag Hesitation is started facing line of dance and finished backing wall diag. The Backward Lock is then danced travelling back diag. to wall. Since the whole movement covers a good deal of ground, it is as well to start it so that it finishes near a corner, the next figure taking you around the corner and along the next line of dance.

Back Whisk

The Back Whisk is a useful movement to end other figures. It can be used to end the Corté, instead of the steps already given. It can also follow the Drag Hesitation and Back Lock or can be danced after the first part of the Natural Turn.

Although a simple figure, the Man must give a firm lead to his partner when he turns her to Whisk position and not lose her contact with his right hip. Care must also be taken whilst turning the Lady to Whisk position not to allow the Man's hold to be disturbed in turning his partner out fan-wise.

Fig. 12. The Whisk position
Note how the heads are turned to follow the line of the body.

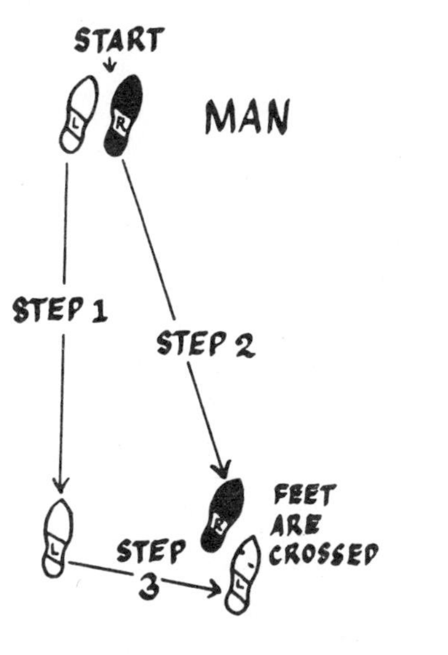

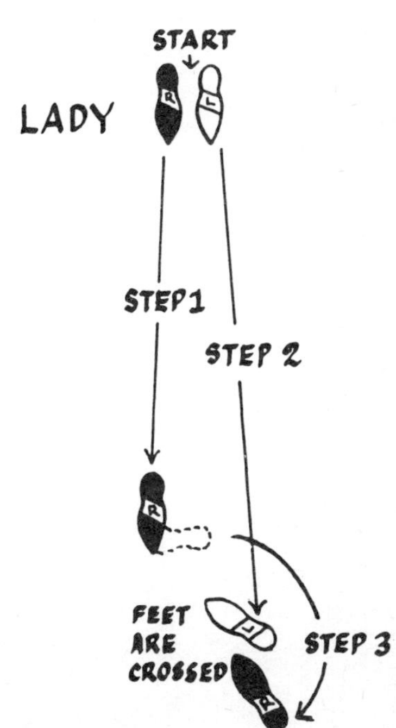

Fig. 13. Back Whisk

A good tip for the Man in avoiding this very common fault, is to *turn in towards his partner* as he turns her to Whisk position. This will correct two faults that can occur:

1. It will help to keep his elbows and arms in line with his back.
2. It will prevent him and his partner opening out at too wide an angle. (*See* Fig.12.)

MAN

Step No.	*Count*
1. Left foot back, bringing partner outside, turning body to left. Toe, then heel.	**1**
2. Right foot to the side and slightly back, at the same time turning partner to Whisk position. Toe.	**2**
3. Whisk left foot behind right foot. Toe, then heel.	**3**
4. Right foot forward in Promenade Position. Heel.	**1**

Note for Man

Lead the Lady into Whisk position by a firm pressure with the base of the right hand, taking care to keep the elbows in line with the back.

Although a slight body turn is made to the right, no turn is made on the actual figure, unless at a corner, or to end the Natural Turn.

LADY

Step No.		*Count*
1.	**Forward right foot outside partner. Heel, then toe.**	**1**
2.	**Turning on the ball of right foot, step to the side and slightly back left foot. Toe.**	**2**
3.	**Continue to turn on ball of left foot, Whisk right foot behind left foot. Toe, then heel.**	**3**
4.	**Left foot forward in Promenade Position. Heel.**	**1**

General Note

An effective 'picture' can be made by the Lady if she uses her head by turning it strongly over her *left* shoulder as she whisks her right foot behind left foot.

Normal Sway and Rise and Fall are used.

Follow with a Syncopated Chassé, as in the Forward Whisk. If used after a Corté, the Chassé will move along the line of dance. If taken after a Back Lock, finish the Back Lock near a corner, take the Whisk into a corner and dance the Chassé along the next line of dance.

Double Reverse Spin

Although Double Reverse Spin is an accepted name for this spinning figure, it is not well named, since it is not a double spin and the action comes under the heading of a toe pivot. It is, however, extremely popular and is used in virtually all dances today, although it originated in the Waltz. There are one or two unusual features in this figure, which is well worth the time spent practising it.

It is one of the few dance figures in which a complete turn is made in one bar of music.

Although the Man only dances three steps to the count of 1, 2, 3, the Lady actually dances four steps, splitting the middle beat and counting 1, 2, *and* 3.

The Lady's steps are quite different to the Man's and he should never attempt to dance it with a partner unless she is familiar with the steps.

It is usually danced facing directly down the line of dance after the last three steps of the Natural Spin Turn (4, 5, 6 of the Reversed Turn) which can be adapted in its amount of turn to enable the Man to face line of dance.

Since it is normally danced with a full turn, it will be finished facing line of dance.

MAN

Step No. *Count*

1. **Left foot forward down line of dance, turning body to left. Heel, then toe.** **1**
2. **Right foot to side across line of dance, still turning. Toe.** **2**
3. **Spinning strongly on the ball of the right foot, close left foot to right foot** *without weight.* **Toe, then heel.** **3**

Continue forward *left* foot into next figure. Heel. Then forward *left* foot into next figure.

LADY

Step No. *Count*

1. **Back right foot down line of dance, turning body to left. Toe, then heel.** **1**
2. **Close left heel to right heel (Heel Turn). Heel, then toe.** **2**
3. **Continue turning on the** ***ball*** **of left foot and step to the side and slightly back with the right foot (small step). Toe.** *and*
4. **Continue to turn on the ball of right foot, cross left foot up in front of right foot. Toe, then heel.** **3**

Back *right* foot into next figure.

Note

This is one of the very few figures in the Waltz

in which the Lady dances a Heel Turn. The Man, therefore, must give a firm lead to the Lady as he takes his 2nd step, otherwise she will assume that her foot goes to the side as in the other Waltz steps.

Do not attempt to use any sway on this figure as the amount and speed of the figure makes it impractical.

The Man rises at the end of the first step and holds the rise until the end of the figure. Lady rises a little later as she has to complete her Heel Turn first.

This figure is usually followed by a Drag Hesitation and Back Lock and thus makes an interesting amalgamation which moves smoothly down the room.

Amalgamations

One of the particular interesting aspects of modern Ballroom dancing, apart from the sheer pleasure of gliding smoothly around the floor to a well-played and attractive tune, is that it allows the dancer to select his own figures according to his mood or his position on the floor.

Whilst there are many figures that can be used, those previously described will be sufficient to enable the average dancer to obtain the utmost enjoyment from his dancing without tying himself in knots!

Having mastered all the figures (and remember that the mastery of a figure means also the ability to guide your partner clearly and confidently into it so that she has no doubt as to what figure she is dancing), the following amalgamations may be a great help.

Remember that every figure has its own alignment and, if kept to, enables the dancer to cover the floor in an orderly manner without endangering the passage of others.

First then, comes an amalgamation of the Basic Turns and Change Steps. Beginners are strongly advised to dance to a simple pattern such as this at first, and in so doing become familiar with the 'Rule of the Road' in the Ballroom.

An Elementary Amalgamation

Commence by facing diag. to wall, with the weight on the right foot.

Note. Try not to start dancing too near a corner, but near the start of a stretch of the room or ballroom floor, or at least halfway. It will give you time to get into the swing of things without having to worry how to negotiate a corner almost immediately.

Start off with a left-foot Closed Change, taking care not to start too near the wall, and go into a Natural Turn. This will finish you facing diag. to centre. Now dance a right-foot Closed Change into a Reverse Turn, to finish facing the wall diag.

If this brings you near a corner, dance a left-foot Closed Change into a Natural Turn, *but only turn very slightly on the last three steps of the Natural Turn.* This will finish you diag. to centre on your next line of dance.

Now dance a right-footed Closed Change into another Reverse Turn. If this brings you near the next corner, dance a left-foot Closed Change and an *underturned* Natural Turn as described above. Having now negotiated two sides of the room, the whole pattern can now be repeated and/or extended if the room is long enough.

By keeping to this simple routine first of all, valuable experience will be gained in using the shape and area of a floor. This will stand you in good stead when you progress to the more advanced figures.

Natural Turn, Reverse Turn, Spin Turn and Natural Hesitation Change

Now try this link-up of figures:

Dance a Natural Turn, Change Step, Reverse

Turn, Change Step, so that it brings you near a corner, facing *into* the corner. Then dance the Natural Spin Turn *around* the corner to finish facing the next line of dance diag. to wall.

Continue with a left-foot Change Step into a Natural Turn, or, if the second side of the room is not wide enough, another Natural Spin Turn to take you round the next corner. Assuming that you have danced a Spin Turn round the *second* corner, you will be facing diag. to wall on the *third* line of dance.

Dance a left-foot Closed Change into a Natural Hesitation Change, which will finish you facing the centre of the room diag. Go straight into a Reverse Turn.

Having now virtually danced round three sides of the room, you can reach your original starting place with either Natural or Reverse Turns, using a Spin Turn at the corners.

Perhaps you have noticed that you are alternating with right or left turns all the time and yet keeping to the shape of the Ballroom.

Natural Turn, Reverse Corté into Back Whisk and Chassé, Natural Spin Turn

Here is an amalgamation of figures that will take you along one side of a small ballroom:

Dance a Natural Turn, Change Step, into the

Reverse Corté, finishing the Corté with a Back Whisk. Finish facing line of dance in Whisk position. Then dance a Chassé into a Spin Turn to take you round the corner.

Natural Spin Turn, Double Reverse Spin, Drag Hesitation and Backward Lock, into Back Whisk.

Here is another amalgamation that, started at one corner on the long side of the room, will take you to the next corner:

Starting at one corner, dance *into* the corner with a Natural Spin Turn, *overturning the last three steps a little more* to face line of dance. Now dance a Double Reverse Spin, using a full turn, and go into a Drag Hesitation finishing backing diag. to wall against the line of dance. Dance the Backward Lock moving diag. to wall. Finish with a Back Whisk into the corner and dance the following Chassé along the next line of dance.

From these suggested groups or amalgamations it will be seen how many different sets of figure can be linked together, and the reader should soon be able to devise amalgamations to suit himself and the room. One warning note: In the thrill of dancing these variations, dancers often make the mistake of using *too many at one time.* A wise dancer always uses *variations* in conjunction with *basic movements.* Just as an experienced chef does not overload a dish with too many ingredients, so the experienced dancer sprinkles his variations lightly amongst the basic figures.

In this way he does not impose too much strain on his partner or himself, and by spacing the more advanced variations between the basic figures, he presents a more balanced and satisfying picture. It is also easier to give attention to other things, such as suiting the figures to the *phrasing* of the music.

No doubt you will have notice by now that I have addressed myself entirely to the Man. This section does in fact concern the Man only. Remember that he does the guiding, the planning and the thinking. The Lady's job is to help him execute that plan by following him and dancing her own steps correctly. However, it must still be remembered that successful Ballroom dancing is the result of a partnership in which each partner can stimulate and inspire the other.

[2]

THE QUICKSTEP

Introduction — Quarter Turns — Natural Turn — Reverse Turn — Lockstep—Natural Spin Turn—Fishtail—Quick Open Reverse Turn — Four-quick Run — Amalgamations

Introduction

Undoubtedly the Quickstep is the most popular of all Ballroom dances today. The quicker tempo, together with the great variety of tunes that can be played — and the adaptable nature of the dance itself — all combine to make this the favourite Ballroom dance.

Although played at varying speeds, the ideal tempo for the Quickstep is about 50 bars per minute. To get the best enjoyment from it, it should be danced to tunes that have a light but steady beat, with the 1st and 2nd bars accented. Rock and Roll music and heavily orchestrated 'swing' numbers are unsuitable for the Quickstep proper.

The Quickstep demands a smooth lightness that only a suitable tune can give it. Other forms of 4/4 rhythm are best enjoyed when dancing Rhythm or Social Dancing (*see* Part II Section 5).

The Construction of the Dance

Basically, the Quickstep consists of walking steps and Chassés.

A 'Chassé' is a step-close-step movement, counted quick, quick slow and is danced in many ways and directions. The 'framework' of the dance, as it were, is the Quarter Turn, which is a figure consisting of Walks and Chassés. As its name implies, it is danced down the room first with a quarter turn to the right, then a quarter turn to the left, thus creating a zig-zag pattern whilst progressing around the floor.

It has its left and right turns, and these are usually commenced with a Chassé type of turn, in which a turn is commenced with a walking step followed by a Chassé movement.

The other steps described give added interest and manoeuvrability to the dance such as the Fishtail, and Four-quick Run. The Quick Open Reverse Turn is an alternative Reverse Turn to the Chassé Reverse Turn and has the advantage of being an 'open' turn.

C.B.M., of course, is used in the Quickstep, but the speed of the dance renders its use less obvious.

Sway is normally used in the Quickstep as for other dances; where it is different an explanation will be given. Rise and Fall, too, is applied in the normal way, and it is interesting to note that both types of Rise are used in the Quickstep. Both the gradual 'spreadover' type of Rise and Fall used in the Waltz, and the sharper, earlier Rise used in the Foxtrot have their place in this popular dance.

Quarter Turns

MAN

Commence facing diag. to wall, weight on left foot.

Step No.	*Count*
1. Forward right foot diag. to wall, turning body to right. Heel, then toe.	**S**
2. Still turning, left foot to side, on same line of dance. Toe.	**Q**
3. Close right foot to left foot, body still turning, now backing diag. to centre. Toe.	**Q**
4. Left foot to side and slightly back. Toe, then heel.	**S**

5. Right foot back diag. to centre, turning body to left. Toe, then heel. S
6. Left foot to side and slightly forward. Toe. Q
7. Close right foot to left foot, now facing diag. to wall. Toe. Q
8. Left foot to side and slightly forward. S

Then forward right foot *outside partner* into next figure.

LADY

Step No. *Count*

1. Left foot back, diag. to wall, turning body to right. Toe, then heel. S
2. Right foot to side, still turning to right. Toe. Q
3. Close left foot to right foot, now facing diag. to centre. Toe. Q
4. Right foot diag. forward. Toe, then heel. S
5. Left foot forward diag. to centre, turning body to left. Heel, then toe. S
6. Right foot to side along line of dance, still turning. Toe. Q
7. Close left foot to right foot, now backing diag. to wall. Toe. Q
8. Right foot to side and slightly back. Toe, then Heel. S

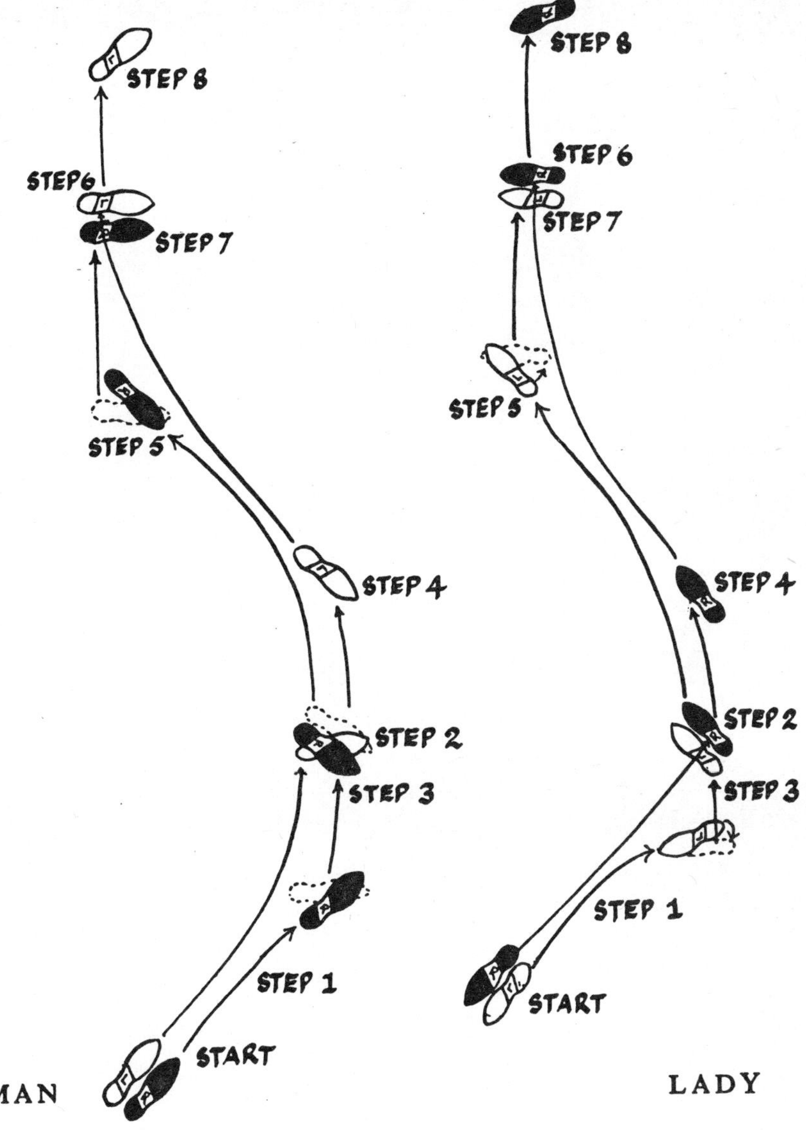

Fig. 14. Quarter Turns

Then backward left foot, partner outside, into next figure.

General Note

Rise and Fall: It is important to remember the type of Rise used in this figure. The Rise is commenced at the end of the 1st step and *continues* until the end of the 4th step, when the heel lowers. The same occurs at the end of the 5th step, the Rise continues to the end of the 8th step, when the heel is lowered and the next step is taken on the heel.

As explained in the chapter on Rise and Fall, this is a gradual, Waltz-type form of Rise. The Lady responds in the same way except that when she feels the body rise at the end of 1 she does not attempt to lift her heel off the ground (*see* page 48).

C.B.M. Since steps 1 and 5 are 'leading' steps, C.B.M. is used on them.

Sway: Slight sway is used on steps 2 and 3, otherwise all steps are straight.

Alignment: Remember that whilst a quarter of a turn is made, first to the left and then to the right, the direction of the whole figure is straight down the room. Remember also that this figure covers a good deal of ground and should not be started too near a corner.

Natural Turn

The Natural Turn in the Quickstep is somewhat similar in pattern to the Natural Hesitation Change in the Waltz and can be used any time the Man is facing diag. to wall. It consists of six steps counted S Q Q S S S and is usually followed by a Chassé Reverse Turn taken diag. to centre.

It is an extremely useful figure and an excellent lead into other Reverse movements. It is best used along the side of a room rather than at a corner.

MAN

Step No.		*Count*
1.	**Forward right foot diag. to wall, turning body to right. Heel, then toe.**	**S**
2.	**Left foot to side still turning right. Toe.**	**Q**
3.	**Close right foot to left still turning to right. Toe, then heel. (Body now backing line of dance.)**	**Q**
4.	**Left foot back, turning body to right. Toe, then heel.**	**S**
5.	**Step to side right foot, body now facing diag. to centre. Heel, then weight felt on inside edge of foot before going on to whole foot.**	**S**
6.	**Brush left foot towards right foot, without weight, before going forward Left foot diag. to centre in a Reverse figure. Heel.**	**S**

Note for Man. The last three steps are all counted *slow,* and firm pressure is needed with the base of the right hand to control your partner and lead her in to the next figure without her automatically changing feet.

Rise and Fall: Down on the 1st step, rising on to the toes during 2 and 3. Down at the end of the 3rd step and no further rise at all. Normal sway on 2 and 3. No further sway.

Special Note. As the 5th step (L.F.) brushes to the right foot, commence to turn the body to the left ready to swing into a left turn.

LADY

Step No.		*Count*
1.	**Left foot back diag. to wall, turning body to right. Toe, then heel.**	**S**
2.	**Right foot to the side, still turning to right. Toe.**	**Q**
3.	**Close left foot to right foot, now facing line of dance. Toe, then heel.**	**Q**
4.	**Right foot forward turning body to right. Heel, then toe.**	**S**
5.	**Left foot to side, now backing diag. centre. Toe, then heel.**	**S**
6.	**Brush right foot to the side of left, without putting weight on it and commence to turn body to left. Toe, then whole foot.**	**S**

Then back right foot diag. to centre, into a Reverse movement. Rise and Fall, and Sway, normal opposite to Man.

Chassé Reverse Turn

The Chassé Reverse Turn should be the first left-hand turn attempted in the Quickstep. It usually follows the Natural Turn, which finishes facing diag. to centre with the left foot free. It should be taken along the room and not too near a corner.

The Chassé Reverse Turn comprises a Chassé type of turn on the first three steps followed by a Progressive Chassé, as at the end of the Quarter Turns. It can be followed by any Natural figure or a Lockstep.

MAN

Step No.	*Count*
1. Left foot forward diag. to centre, turning body to left. Heel, then toe.	**S**
2. Right foot to side, still turning to left. Toe.	**Q**
3. Close left foot to right foot, turning to left to end backing line of dance. Toe, then heel.	**Q**
4. Right foot back, turning body to left. Toe, then heel.	**S**

5. **Left foot to side, still turning body to left. Toe.** **Q**
6. **Close right foot to left foot. Now facing diag. to wall. Toe.** **Q**
7. **Left foot to side and slightly forward. Toe, then heel.** **S**
8. **Right foot forward outside partner, diag. to wall. Heel.** **S**

LADY

Step No.	*Count*
1. **Right foot back diag. to centre, turning body to left. Toe, then heel.**	**S**
2. **Left foot to side, still turning to left. Toe.**	**Q**
3. **Close right foot to left foot. Now facing line of dance. Toe, then heel.**	**Q**
4. **Left foot forward, turning body to left. Heel, then toe.**	**S**
5. **Right foot to side still turning body to left. Toe.**	**Q**
6. **Close left foot to right foot. Now back diag. to wall. Toe.**	**Q**
7. **Right foot to side and slightly back. Toe, then heel.**	**S**
8. **Left foot back, diag. to wall, partner outside. Toe.**	**S**

General Notes

Normal technique is used on all steps. The rules governing C.B.M., Sway, Rise and Fall, etc., apply as in all other basic figures. Three-quarters of a turn is made over the whole figure.

Lockstep

The Lockstep is a useful figure, since it allows a couple to progress along the room after dancing such figures as the Quarter Turn and the Chassé Reverse Turn. It also demonstrates the ability of the Man to dance a series of steps whilst outside his partner without losing contact at the hips.

It is, in effect, a Chassé taken along the room, but crossing the feet instead of closing them. Since the Lockstep covers a fair amount of ground, it is not wise to start it too near a corner, or the Man will find himself dancing straight into the corner and leaving no room to turn.

MAN

Step No.		*Count*
1.	**Right foot forward, diag. to wall, outside partner. Heel, then toe.**	**S**
2.	**Left foot diag. forward. Toe.**	**Q**
3.	**Cross right foot behind left foot. Toe.**	**Q**
4.	**Left foot diag. forward. Toe, then heel.**	**S**
5.	**Right foot forward, diag. to wall, outside partner. Heel.**	**S**

Fig. 15. Lockstep

LADY

Step No.	*Count*
1. Left foot back diag. to wall. Toe, then heel.	**S**
2. Right foot back. Toe.	**Q**
3. Cross left foot in front of right foot. Toe.	**Q**
4. Right foot diag. back. Toe, then heel.	**S**
5. Left foot back, diag. to wall, partner outside. Toe.	**S**

General Notes

Rise at the end of the 1st step and lower at the end of the 4th step. C.B.M. is used when stepping outside partner. No Sway is used and no turn made.

Step 5, of course, becomes the 1st step of any Natural figure.

Natural Spin Turn

The Natural Spin Turn in the Quickstep is almost the same as the Turn of the same name in the Waltz, except, of course, for its timing and its ending, which is a Progressive Chassé (commencing with step 7).

Best used at a corner, it need not cover a lot of ground; indeed, the more compact the actual

Pivot and Spin is danced, the easier it will be to master. Remember, as in the Waltz, to use the body strongly on step 4 to enable both Lady and Man to pivot easily.

If danced at a corner, the Chassé ending can be danced towards the centre of the room on the next line of dance and followed by a Quick Open Reverse Turn. This can be a very attractive and enjoyable amalgamation.

MAN

Step No.		*Count*
1,2,3.	**First three steps of the Natural Turn, to end backing line of dance. (1) Heel, then toe. (2) Toe. (3) Toe, then heel.**	**SQQ**
4.	**Left foot back (medium length) turning body strongly to right keeping right foot extended forward in front of left foot. End facing line of dance. Toe, then heel, then toe.**	**S**
5.	**Extend right foot slightly forward down line of dance, still turning to right. Heel, then toe.**	**S**
6.	**Continue turning to right and step to side and slightly back with left foot. Now backing diag. to centre. Toe, then heel.**	**S**

Finish with steps 5 to 9 of the Quarter Turns (Progressive Chassé).

LADY

Step No.		*Count*
1,2,3.	**First three steps of the Natural Turn, now facing line of dance. (1) Toe, then heel. (2) Toe. (3) Toe, then heel.**	**SQQ**
4.	**Right foot forward, turning body to right. Heel, then toe.**	**S**
5.	**Left foot back and leftwards, still turning to right. Toe.**	**S**
6.	**Continuing to turn right on ball of left foot, brush right foot to left foot and then step diag. forward with right foot. Now facing diag. to centre. Toe, then then heel.**	**S**

Finish with steps 5 to 9 of the Quarter Turns (Progressive Chassé).

General Notes

Rise at the end of the 1st step, lower at end of 3. No Rise on the Pivot. Rise at the end of 5, lower at the end of 6.

Normal Sway and C.B.M. (strong C.B.M. on steps 4 and 5).

The Fishtail

Here is a very jolly and interesting figure, which, once you have learnt the Lockstep, should prove quite easy.

A rough description of this figure would be that of two consecutive Locksteps with each one executed with different feet. It can be danced, as with the Lockstep, any time the Man is stepping outside his partner with his right foot, as at the end of the Quarter Turns.

Care must be taken to give your partner a clear indication that it is a Fishtail and *not* a Lockstep, since the actual crossing step occurs on the first 'Quick' and not the second as in the Lockstep. This is done by relaxing the right knee on the 1st step, together with a turn of the body to the left as step 1 is taken, then turn body to right as the left foot crosses behind.

It is a movement of six steps counted, SQQQ QS and is commenced facing line of dance or diag. to centre and is finished facing diag. wall.

Like other 'travelling' steps, it should not be started too near a corner because of the distance travelled during the figure.

MAN

Step No.		*Count*
1.	**Right foot forward outside partner, taking the right leg leftwards well across the body and turning slightly leftwards. Heel, then toe.**	**S**
2.	**Rising to the toe on the right foot and turning the body to the right, cross left foot behind right foot. Toe.**	**Q**
3.	**Small step forward right foot and slightly to the right.**	**Q**
4.	**Left foot diag. forward, left shoulder leading.**	**Q**
5.	**Cross right foot loosely behind left foot.**	**Q**
6.	**Left foot diag. forward.**	**S**

Finish movement by stepping forward right foot outside partner into any Natural figure.

LADY

Step No.		*Count*
1.	**Back left foot, partner outside, taking leg well under body and turning body slightly left. Toe, then heel.**	**S**
2.	**Turning body to right cross right foot in front of left. Toe.**	**Q**
3.	**Back left foot (small step) and slightly to left. Toe.**	**Q**

4. Right foot diag. back, right shoulder leading. Toe. **Q**
5. Cross left foot loosely in front of right. **Q**
6. Right foot diag. back. Toe, then heel. **S**

General Notes

Relax the knee of the first step a little more than usual and rise rather sharply into the first crossing movement.

'Left shoulder leading' needs a little explanation as it is the first time the expression has been used. In the case of the Man, as he crosses his left foot behind his right, he turns strongly to the right and thus creates a position whereby his left shoulder is forward over his right foot. This position should be held until the end of the 5th step. The Lady does the normal opposite.

This shoulder-leading position, together with the first step taken strongly across the body, enables both Man and Lady to dance a figure of six steps outside each other without losing contact at the hips, and is an important factor in the neat execution of the figure.

Also, the rising to the toes having been made on the 2nd step the legs should be kept well braced throughout the four Quicks to avoid a 'bouncing' movement.

Quick Open Reverse Turn

This is a useful figure for travelling down the room, since it is also ended by dancing either a Progressive Chassé or a Four-quick Run.

It can be preceded by a Natural Turn finishing diag. to centre, but the most popular and free-moving ending is undoubtedly the Progressive Chassé to centre taken at the end of a Natural Spin Turn, when the latter figure is used to turn a corner.

This enables the Chassé ending and the Quick Open Reverse Turn to be danced along the side of a room without fear of being brought up short near a corner.

MAN

Step No.		*Count*
1.	**Left foot forward, diag. to centre, turning body to left. Heel, then toe.**	**S**
2.	**Right foot to the side, still turning, on the same line of dance, allowing the Lady to move more to the Man's right side, so that the next step is taken with the Lady outside her partner. Toe.**	**Q**
3.	**Left foot back down line of dance with** *left leg well under the body,* **bringing partner outside. Toe, then heel.**	**Q**

4. Right foot back, in line with partner, turning body to left. Toe, then heel. S

Follow with a Four-quick Run or Progressive Chassé.

LADY

Step No. *Count*

1. Back right foot diag. to centre, turning body to left. Toe, then heel. S

2. Left foot to the side and slightly forward pointing along the line of dance. Toe. Q

3. Right foot forward down line of dance, outside partner. Toe, then heel. Q

4. Left foot forward, turning body to left, in line with partner. Heel. S

Note for Lady

This turn is actually an 'open' or Foxtrot type of turn, where the Lady's steps usually take the form of a Heel Turn. In this, however, the speed of the turn renders a Heel Turn difficult and so on the 2nd step the Lady takes a small step to the side of the right foot and points it into position down the line of dance.

Care must also be taken by the Lady to keep her hips well forward and in contact with her partner as he takes his 3rd step outside her, otherwise a bad body line will result. Nothing looks worse in modern Ballroom dancing than to see an outside step taken with 'daylight' showing between the partners (*see* Figs. 2 and 3).

General Notes

If the Quick Open Reverse Turn is danced following a Progressive Chassé to the centre of the room, the last step of the Progressive Chassé will be taken outside partner. A good firm lead, therefore, is necessary, together with a strong body swing to the left on the 1st step of the turn, so that the Lady is well in line as the turn is commenced.

C.B.M., Rise and Fall, and Sway, are all used normally and three-eighths of a turn is normally used over the four steps.

The reader may wonder why the figure is called a *Quick* Open Reverse Turn. There is a similar type of turn which was danced with all four steps counted slow and resembled a Foxtrot turn; it has now fallen into disuse as being quite unsuitable to the Quickstep.

The Four-quick Run

(Taken after a Quick Open Reverse Turn)

MAN

Commence as at the end of a Quick Open Reverse Turn, with the right foot back down line of dance with body turned strongly to left, partner in line.

Step No. *Count*

1. **To the side and slightly forward left foot, diag. to wall preparing to step outside partner. Toe. Q**
2. **Right foot forward (small step). Toe. Q**
3. **Left foot diag. forward, outside partner. Toe. Q**
4. **Cross right foot rather loosely behind left foot. Toe. Q**
5. **Left foot diag. forward, preparing to step outside partner. Toe, then heel. S**

Note for Man

Rise and Fall: The 1st step is taken on the toe, the Rise having commenced from the previous step. All the steps are then taken on the toes, lowering at the end of the 5th step.

No sway is used on this figure and no turn used. The figure is dancing diag. to wall throughout.

It is followed by any figure starting diag. to wall on the right foot.

LADY

Commence with left foot forward down line of dance, turning left.

Step No. *Count*

1. **Right foot to side and slightly back (body backing wall). Toe. Q**

2. Small step back left foot diag. to wall, partner outside. Toe. Q
3. Right foot diag. back. Q
4. Cross left foot in front of right (rather loosely). Q
5. Right foot diag. back. Toe, then heel. S

Rise and Fall, Sway and other details, as Man.

Note for Lady

As the 1st step is taken, not too much body turn must be made to the left, since this will tend to cause lack of contact at the hips.

General Notes

If this figure is going to be used following a Quick Open Reverse Turn, make sure that it is not started too far down the room. It covers a good deal of ground and sufficient space should be allowed for it along the side of the room.

The Four-quick Run can also be danced after the 5th step of the Quarter Turns taken back diag. to centre. In this case, not so much body turn will be used as only a quarter of a turn is danced.

When practising this step, do not attempt to take too long a step. Concentrate more on getting four light, well-braced steps, high on the toes.

The Four-quick Run used at a corner

It sometimes happens that a Quarter Turn or

Lockstep will be finished too near a corner to allow even a Spin Turn to be used. In this case the following is an excellent way of dancing along the next line of dance by using the Four-quick Run.

As the right foot is taken forward outside partner at the end of the Quarter Turn or Lockstep, *check* on that foot, without turning, and step back on to the back (left) foot. Then back right foot, turning to face diag. to the wall of the next line of dance, and dance the Four-quick Run along the new line.

This is a very useful figure in a crowded room and one that can be thoroughly recommended.

Amalgamations

The speedier nature of the Quickstep renders it imperative that the figures are neatly linked together so that the flow of the dance does not impede other dancers.

All the figures shown previously are designed to fit smoothly into the shape of a room and the following amalgamations will be of great help in planning a progressive pattern around the floor.

Elementary Groups (Suitable for a small ballroom floor or studio.)

Commence with the Quarter Turns and Lockstep. If at a corner by then, dance a Spin Turn around the corner with a Progressive Chassé ending, in to another Spin Turn at the second corner.

Dance the Progressive Chassé ending along the third line of dance and go into a Natural Turn and Chassé Reverse Turn.

This simple linking of basic figures should be thoroughly mastered before attempting other groups and should be thought of as the framework of the Quickstep.

It is a good plan always to drop back, as it were, to a basic figure or group of figures after dancing some more advanced variations. In this way the dance does not become overloaded with advanced figures, until, in desperation, you are forced to slow down or crash into another couple!

Having danced the above without mishap and as smoothly as possible, try the following:

Quarter Turns, Lockstep, check to Four-quick Run into Spin Turn at a corner.

Another group for a long side of the room is:

Spin Turn at a corner, Chassé to centre into Quick Open Reverse Turn and Four-quick Run into a Spin Turn at the next corner.

Now try this amalgamation:

Quarter Turns into Fishtail, Natural Turn (if

at a corner), then dancing the Chassé Reverse Turn along the next line of dance and checking at the second corner. Dance a Four-quick Run along the third line of dance into a Quarter Turn, Lockstep and Spin Turn.

This will bring you almost to where you started with the aid of a Progressive Chassé ending to the Spin Turn, and the whole routine could be danced again.

Although I have suggested some groupings here, there are many other ways in which the steps shown can be linked together and thus provide a very interesting variety of amalgamations that should satisfy most dancers and at the same time be enjoyable because they are not too complicated.

Remember: *Always* space out your variations with the basic figures and at all times keep to your correct alignment. This will enable you to thread your way in and out of even a crowded ballroom without leaving a swathe of battered couples in your wake! Practice will enable you to 'gauge' the distance a figure or amalgamation will take.

Try not to start any progressive figure too near a corner or you may find yourself hurtling into it with no room to extricate yourselves.

Always keep a weather eye open for your neighbours when dancing. Keeping your head and eyes turned left can help considerably in allowing you to assess the room that is available and help you to decide what figure you are going to dance. Don't, whatever you do, attempt a figure without knowing what is in front of you. Even profuse apologies do not compensate for a ruined stocking!

[3]

THE FOXTROT

Introduction — Three-Step — Natural Turn — Reverse Turn — Change of Direction Step — Impetus Turn — Whisk — Weave — Natural Telemark — Amalgamations

Introduction

The Foxtrot is not an easy dance to master and for that reason the beginner should learn the Waltz and Quickstep thoroughly before attempting it.

The smooth gliding steps of the Foxtrot look deceptively simple when danced by an adept, but that smoothness and the gradual merging of one step with another is only acquired after a good deal of practice.

These things must be said, in case the reader, looking at the simple descriptions, is tempted to assume that it is easier than the other dances.

Before learning any of the steps, it would be as well if the all-important chapter on the 'Walk' be read through thoroughly once more, so that the smooth, gliding walking action is clearly understood, since this action applies to all progressive 'slow' steps in the Foxtrot.

Truly the description of the Foxtrot as the 'Classic' of all the dances is an apt one. All that we have learnt about smoothness, style, grace, balance and control has been brought about by past study of the Foxtrot.

Whilst the carefree dancer will be content to Waltz and Quickstep without paying too much attention to the various technical points like footwork, C.B.M., Sway, etc., these are an essential part of the Foxtrot. Without them it becomes meaningless and without style. Style is essential to its satisfactory execution.

But when all that is said, the reader who feels that he would like to learn to dance with a degree of competence, should undoubtedly tackle the Foxtrot.

The basic of the dance is the Feather Step and the Three-Step, and all turns are of the 'open' or passing variety.

The Lady should pay careful attention to her steps in the turns. These are known as Heel Turns and are danced by turning on the heel of one foot and then transferring the weight to the other. Since normally the Lady dancer will be wearing high heels, it will be seen that this enables the turn to be made by the Lady in a very tiny space, thus allowing the Man to perform his smooth passing 'open' turn without anything happening to destroy the flow of his movement.

With regard to the technical points to watch, the following general principles should be borne in mind.

C.B.M. All 'leading' steps, that is the 1st and 4th steps of all turns, are taken using C.B.M., both Man and Lady, unless otherwise mentioned.

Also the slow steps in the Feather Step and Three-Step are taken with C.B.M. *and the 3rd step of* the Feather Step and the 6th step of the Reverse Turn are always taken in C.B.M.P., that is with the leg taken across or under the other leg to maintain contact with partner when stepping outside.

Sway. There are very few exceptions to the following rule. If a step has been taken forward on the right foot when dancing a slow step, you *Sway to the right on the following two quick steps.* A forward slow step on the left foot is followed by a Sway to the left on the following two quick steps.

The rule applies to the backward steps as well,

so that the Lady does the exact counterpart to the Man. Any exceptions to this rule will be explained.

It will be found, as one becomes a more experienced dancer, that if a strong forward or backward body 'thrust' is used on all leading steps, it will feel quite natural to sway towards that foot on the succeeding two quick steps.

Rise and Fall: The general rule is as follows: In the slow, quick, quick, movement that is constantly recurring in the Foxtrot, the Rise is taken at the end of the slow step and held until the end of the 3rd step. It is, however, still a gradual movement and the peak of the Rise is not felt until the second quick is taken.

This is where the use of the knees is of paramount importance. If the Rise is taken abruptly at the end of the 1st step, without relaxing the knee slightly to take the strain, an extremely stilted action will result.

A good way of thinking of the use of the knees to obtain a smooth Rise and Fall, is to compare them with the shock absorbers on a car. The shock absorbers enable a car to go over bumps or hollows in a road whilst keeping the body of the car gliding smoothly along on an even keel. When you see a couple dancing stiffly you will know that they have not appreciated the shock-absorbing qualities of the knees!

Alignment: Although the pattern follows that of the other dances — in a zig-zag or diagonal pattern around the floor — there is much more progression in the Foxtrot than in any other dance.

For example, a simple amalgamation consisting of Feather Step, Three-Step, Natural Turn will cover up to twenty-seven feet of floor, or half the size of a normal ballroom! Care must, therefore, be taken in selecting not only the figures used, but the position on the floor from which they can be started.

It follows that the Foxtrot needs a good deal of floor space and is seen to its best advantage in competitions and medal tests, where the circumstances (and space!) are usually favourable.

Feather Step

One of the characteristics of the Foxtrot is the smooth integration of one figure into another. For that reason it will be found that the last step of one figure, as shown in the descriptions, becomes the first step of another.

Thus, the Feather Step is always used as a 'lead' in to a Reverse figure and the last step of the Feather Step becomes the first step of, say, a Rverse Turn.

The Feather Step is commenced diag. to centre and can be slightly curved so that the following Reverse figure is taken almost down the line of dance.

MAN

Step No.		*Count*
1.	**Right foot forward. Heel, then toe.**	**S**
2.	**Left foot forward preparing to step outside partner. Toe.**	**Q**
3.	**Right foot forward outside partner on partner's right side. Toe, then heel. (In C.B.M.P.)**	**Q**
4.	**Left foot forward in line with partner, turning body to left. Heel.**	**S**

LADY

Step No.		*Count*
1.	**Left foot back, turning body to right. Toe, then heel.**	**S**
2.	**Right foot back. Toe, then heel.**	**Q**
3.	**Left foot back, partner now outside. Toe, then heel. (In C.B.M.P.)**	**Q**
4.	**Right foot back, turning body to left. Toe, then heel.**	**S**

General Note

There are no exceptions to the normal technique applied as explained in the opening section on the Foxtrot.

Reverse Turn

It is a good plan to start dancing the Foxtrot with a Feather Step, followed by a Reverse Turn taken diag. to centre. It should be noted that although this is a figure of seven steps, the 1st step is also the last step of the preceding Feather Step.

The Reverse Turn consists of an 'open' type of turn followed by a Feather Step started backward (known as a 'Feather Finish').

Three-quarters of a turn is made over the whole figure and it is finished facing the wall diag. It can be followed by a Three-Step, or a Whisk if near a corner.

MAN

Step No.		*Count*
1.	**Left foot forward diag. to centre, turning body to left. Heel, then toe.**	**S**
2.	**Right foot to side across line of dance, still turning to left. Toe.**	**Q**
3.	**Left foot back, down line of dance. Toe, then heel.**	**Q**

4. **Right foot back, turning body to left. Toe, then heel, then toe.** **S**
5. **Left foot to side and slightly forward, preparing to step outside partner. Toe.** **Q**
6. **Right foot forward outside partner on partner's right side. Toe, then heel. (In C.B.M.P.)** **Q**
7. **Left foot forward, in line with partner, diag. to wall, turning body slightly to left. Heel.** **S**

LADY

Step No.	*Count*
1. **Right foot back diag. to centre, turning body to left. Toe, then heel.**	**S**
2. **Close left foot to right foot, still turning to left on heel of right foot to end feet together facing line of dance. Heel, then toe.**	**Q**
3. **Right foot forward. Toe, then heel.**	**Q**
4. **Left foot forward, turning body to left. Heel, then toe.**	**S**
5. **Right foot to side, still turning to left. Toe, then heel.**	**Q**
6. **Left foot back diag. to wall, partner outside on right side. Toe, then heel. (In C.B.M.P.)**	**Q**

7. **Right foot back diag. to wall, turning body slightly to left. Toe.** **S**

General Notes

Normal technique is used—as explained previously—throughout the figure. The Lady will notice that the actual Heel Turn is danced quite naturally on the heels of *both feet* and, unlike the Man, she will not rise until the end of the 2nd step, but will brace her body at the end of the 1st step.

Three-Step

The Three-Step is regarded as the 'link' step of the Foxtrot. It connects the Reverse and Natural Turns, and in fact acts as a link between all Reverse and Natural figures.

Although shown as a figure of three steps, the last step(s) is always the first of the next figure.

Notice, too, that the 1st step, although counted quick, is taken on the heel, a departure from normal technique. That is because it follows a slow step from the preceding figure, from which there is no tendency to rise. The step is therefore taken on the heel followed by an immediate Rise.

The Three-Step needs a good deal of practice to develop the smoothness essential to the correct performance of the figure.

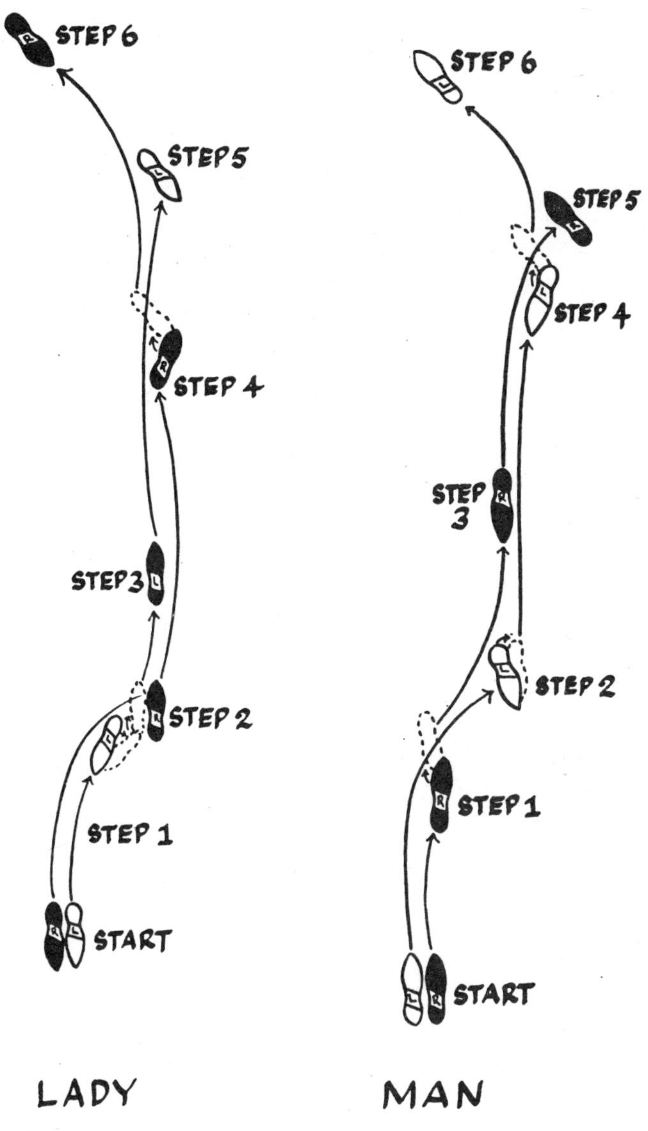

Fig. 16. The Natural Turn, showing the 'open' type of turn (Man) and the Lady's Heel turn.

MAN

Step No.	*Count*
1. Right foot forward. Heel, then toe.	**Q**
2. Left foot forward. Toe, then heel.	**Q**
3. Right foot forward. Heel.	**S**

LADY

Step No.	*Count*
1. Left foot back. Toe, then heel.	**Q**
2. Right foot back. Toe, then heel.	**Q**
3. Left foot back. Toe, then heel.	**S**

General Notes

C.B.M. on the 3rd step. *Sway* to the left on steps 1 and 2 (this is created from the C.B.M. used on the preceding step).

Rise at the end of the 1st step, lower at the end of the 2nd step. Down on the last step.

Natural Turn

The timing of the Natural Turn is different from the basic slow, quick quick 'impulses', characteristic of most Foxtrot figures, in that the timing is counted SQQSSS. It consists of an 'open' turn, followed by a 'Pull Step'.

It is best used at a corner, and allows the learner to negotiate a corner successfully and dance a Feather Step along the next line of dance.

Particular attention should be shown to the footwork as described, to obtain the feeling of 'pulling' one foot towards the other.

The Natural Turn is often superseded by the Impetus Turn but it is a very useful turn to learn, requiring a good deal of control, so necessary to the correct interpretation of the Foxtrot.

It will be noticed also that the steps 4, 5 and 6, being slow steps are taken with no Rise at all. The Lady does not dance a Heel Pull, as the Man does, but dances the Lady's equivalent, a 'Brush Step' (somewhat similar to the Waltz).

MAN

Step No.		*Count*
1.	**Right foot forward towards line of dance turning body to right. Heel, then toe.**	**S**
2.	**Left foot to side across line of dance, still turning to right. Toe.**	**Q**
3.	**Right foot back down line of dance. Toe, then heel.**	**Q**
4.	**Left foot back, turning body to right. Toe, then heel.**	**S**
5.	**Pull right foot to side of left foot, small step, still turning to right on heel of left foot—foot flat. Now facing diag. to centre. Heel, then inside edge to whole foot, then flat.**	**S**

6. **Brush left foot to right foot then step forward left foot diag. to centre, turning body slightly to left. Inside edge of foot to heel of left foot.** **S**

This figure may be commenced facing diag. to wall.

LADY

Step No.	*Count*
1. **Left foot back down line of dance turning body to right. Toe, then heel.**	**S**
2. **Close right to left foot, still turning to right on heel of left foot to end feet together facing line of dance. Heel, then toe.**	**Q**
3. **Left foot forward. Toe, then heel.**	**Q**
4. **Right foot forward, turning body to right. Heel, then toe.**	**S**
5. **Left foot to side, still turning to right. Now backing diag. to centre. Toe, then heel, then inside edge of right foot.**	**S**
6. **Brush right foot to left foot and then step back right foot. Toe.**	**S**

This figure may be commenced backing diag. to wall.

General Notes

C.B.M. on steps 1, 4 and 6. Sway to the right on 2 and 3, Sway on 5 to the left, straight on 6.

Normal Rise and Fall on steps 1, 2 and 3. No further Rise.

The Natural Turn is normally followed by a Feather Step.

Change of Direction

The Change of Direction Step in the Foxtrot is an extremely useful figure.

It enables a couple to change their direction in a very small space. Up to half a turn can be made over the three steps and can be danced any time the left foot is free when facing diag. to wall or at a corner.

It needs a little practice to get the feel of the sideways gliding action between the 1st and 2nd steps and for that reason it is important to note the edge-of-foot technique described below. The Man must give a strong lead with his body and the base of his right hand to indicate to his partner what figure is being danced.

Note the all-slow timing and the lack of Rise and Fall.

MAN

Step No.	*Count*
1. Left foot forward diag. to wall, turning body to left. Heel.	**S**

2. **Right foot diag. forward with right side of body leading, then turn left on right foot, close left foot to right foot (slightly forward), keeping weight on right foot. Now facing diag. to centre. Inside edge of toe, heel of right foot, then inside edge of toe of left foot.** **S**
3. **Left foot forward, diag. to centre. Heel.** **S**

LADY

Step No. *Count*

1. **Right foot back, diag. to wall, turning body to left. Toe, then heel.** **S**
2. **Left foot diag. back, with left side of body leading, then turn left on left foot and close right foot to left foot (slightly back), keeping weight on left foot. Now backing diag. to centre. Toe, inside edge of toe, heel, then inside edge of toe of right foot.** **S**
3. **Right foot back diag. to centre. Toe.** **S**

General Notes

The feet are kept flat throughout the movement although the inside edge of the toe is used at the end of the 2nd step of Man to control the movement.

Sway to the left on the 2nd step, but straighten as the left foot brushes to the right foot as it is taken forward. C.B.M. is used on the 1st and 3rd steps.

The Change of Direction Step is usually followed by a Feather Step.

Impetus Turn

The Impetus Turn can safely be referred to as the 'Spin Turn' of the Foxtrot. Its pattern is roughly the same and its function (that of negotiating a corner) the same as in the Waltz and the Quickstep.

It has the additional advantage of having a S Q Q rhythm throughout and is more popular than the basic Natural Turn for that reason. It consists of the first three steps of a Natural Turn followed by a form of Heel Turn danced by the Man and ends with a Feather Finish. It can be danced after a Three-Step when facing line of dance or diag. to wall.

The 'Impetus' that it gets its name from is the strong body turn made at the end of the 1st step and will result in the turn being continued on the right foot.

MAN

Commence by dancing steps 1, 2 and 3 of the Natural Turn.

Step No.	*Count*
1. Left foot back down line of dance, turning body to right. Toe, then heel.	**S**
2. Close right foot to left foot, turning to right on heel of right foot. Now facing diag. to centre. Heel, then toe.	**Q**
3. Left foot to side and slightly back, still turning body to right. Now backing diag. to centre against line of dance. Toe, then heel.	**Q**
4. Right foot back diag. to centre against line of dance. Toe.	**S**

Note: Follow with steps 5, 6 and 7 of the Reverse Turn, which is the Feather Finish.

LADY

Taken after 3rd step of Natural Turn.

Step No.	*Count*
1. Right foot forward down line of dance, turning body to right. Heel, then toe.	**S**
2. Left foot to side, still turning to right. Now backing diag. to centre. Toe.	**Q**
3. Continuing to turn on toe of left foot, brush right foot to left foot then step with right foot diag. forward. Now facing diag. to centre against the line of dance. Toe, then heel.	**Q**

4. Left foot forward diag. to centre against the line of dance. Heel. **S**

Note: Follow this figure with steps 5, 6 and 7 of the Reverse Turn, which is the Feather Finish.

General Notes

Normal technique on 1, 2, 3, of the Natural Turn. Strong C.B.M. on the 1st step of the Impetus. Slight Sway on the 2nd step. Rise at the end of the 2nd step, lower at the end of the 3rd step.

The Impetus Turn can be followed by any Reverse or left foot figure.

The Whisk

The Whisk can also be used to effect in the Foxtrot as well as the Waltz.

It can be used in place of the Change of Direction Step and serves the same purpose. It can be danced any time the left foot is free facing diag. to wall or at a corner and is followed by a Feather Finish started from a Whisk (or Promenade) Position.

Normal technique is observed throughout and apart from the earlier Foxtrot type of Rise is identical to the Waltz Whisk.

MAN

Step No.		*Count*
1.	Forward left foot diag. to wall. Heel, then toe.	S
2.	Right foot to the side and slightly forward, preparing to turn partner to Whisk Position. Toe.	Q
3.	Turning partner to Whisk Position cross left foot behind right foot, now facing along line of dance (or new line of dance if at a corner). Toe, then heel.	Q
4.	Forward right foot in Promenade Position and dance a Feather Step (turning Lady square to partner between steps 1 and 2 of the Feather Step). Heel, then toe.	SQQS

LADY

Step No.		*Count*
1.	Back right foot. Toe, then heel.	S
2.	Left foot back and to the side, body turning to the right. Toe.	Q
3.	Cross right foot behind left still turning, now in Whisk Position. Toe, then heel.	Q
4.	Forward left foot in Promenade Position and dance a Feather Step, turning square to partner. Heel, then toe.	SQQS

General Notes

As the 3rd step crosses behind right (as Lady) the head may be turned strongly either to the right or the left (although it is better for balance to turn the head to the left).

The Weave

The Weave is a truly typical Foxtrot figure, admirably suited to its rhythm. It also provides an alternative to the S Q Q rhythm of most Foxtrot figures, since the figure contains, at one point, six quick steps in succession.

As the name suggests it is a weaving-like pattern and is taken after the first four steps of a Reverse Turn, when, instead of continuing into a Feather Finish, the Man checks his movement on the 4th step and then steps forward slightly against the line of dance into the Weave movement.

The Lady's steps are the normal opposite and the usual technique applies to most of the steps.

The Weave has the greatest number of steps of any figure in the Foxtrot and it is therefore somewhat lengthy. Care should be taken to see that enough floor space is available before attempting the movement. It can be commenced either facing line of dance or diag. to centre, and ends with a Feather Finish.

To give an overall picture of the step it can be described as the first four steps of the Reverse Turn, checking on the 4th step, followed by the four quick steps of the Weave and ending with a Feather Finish.

To give an overall picture of the step it can be described as the first four steps of the Reverse Turn, checking on the 4th step, followed by the four quick steps of the Weave and ending with a Feather Finish.

MAN

Step No.		*Count*
1 to 4.	**Dance the first four steps of the Reverse Turn making a three-eighths-turn (as the 4th step is taken back down the line of dance or diag. to wall, allow the knee to relax and the right heel lower to the floor).**	**S Q Q S**
	Now in the Weave:	
5.	**Extend left foot forward against line of dance, turning body slightly to the left. Heel, then toe.**	**Q**
6.	**Small step to the side, right foot still turning slightly, body now backing diag. diag. to centre. Toe.**	**Q**

7. **Back left foot, diag. to centre** *bringing partner outside.* **Toe.** **Q**
8. **Back right foot, turning body to left,** *partner in line.* **Toe (but allowing heel to relax slightly).** **Q**

9 to 11. Dance the last three steps of a Reverse Turn (the Feather Finish). **Q Q S**

LADY

Step No. *Count*

1 to 4. Dance the first four steps of the Reverse Turn finishing left foot forward on heel, relaxing left knee and allowing the body to check. Then into Weave. **S Q Q S**

5. **Back right foot, small step, turning body to left. Toe then heel.** **Q**
6. **Small step to side left foot. Toe.** **Q**
7. **Right foot forward** *outside partner.* **Toe.** **Q**
8. **Left foot forward, turning body to left, in line with partner. Toe.** **Q**

9 to 11. End with the last three steps of the Feather Finish. **Q Q S**

General Notes

It will thus be seen that by combining the four quick steps of the Weave and the two quick steps of the Feather Finish, a succession of six quick steps are danced.

Care therefore, must be taken to dance these six 'quicks' lightly on the toes with well braced legs to avoid a 'bouncing' effect. Man rises at the end of the 1st quick and stays up on the toes until the end of the 6th quick, although (as shown) he has a slight relaxing of the knees at the end of step 8, before carrying on into the Feather Finish.

Strong C.B.M. is used on step 4 and step 8 for both Man and Lady.

Sway to left on steps 5 and 6 (Lady opposite).

Alignment is roughly that of the Reverse Turn and a three-quarter turn is made over the whole figure.

This step is worth mastering for the sense of leg control gained in dancing six quick steps in succession as lightly as possible.

Natural Telemark

Once the basic turns are thoroughly understood and mastered, there is no doubt that the Natural Telemark is an extremely useful alternative to other Natural Turns. One of the reasons is that three-quarters of a turn is made on only three steps, an advantage on a crowded floor.

The figure is ended by a type of Feather Step called a Hover Feather, so called because of the hover effect at the start caused by the ending of

Natural Telemark and the omission of the first slow step of the ordinary Feather Step.

The Telemark is another movement that has more than two 'quicks' in succession; in this case four quicks are made of the last two steps of the Natural Telemark and the first two of the Hover Feather.

A good deal of body and partner control by the Man is needed to lead the Lady into this step but it is well worth the time spent, and is a useful addition to the Foxtrot repertoire.

Starting position as for any Natural Turn or at a corner.

MAN

Step No.		*Count*
1.	**Forward right foot diag. to wall, turning body to right. Heel, then toe.**	**S**
2.	**Still turning strongly, step to the side with the left foot across line of dance and well round partner. Toe.**	**Q**
3.	**Step to the side right foot, continuing to turn on the ball of left foot to finish facing diag. to centre. Toe.**	**Q**

Owing to the amount of turn and the force behind making three-quarters of a turn over three steps, it will be found that as the weight is taken on 3rd step (right foot), the body will continue to turn slightly and the left foot will tend to veer into, or hover towards, the right foot.

The left foot is then replaced to the side and slightly forward into the Hover Feather thus:

4. Left foot to the side and slightly forward with a strong left shoulder lead, preparing to step outside partner, diag. to centre. Toe. **Q**

5. Right foot forward outside partner. Toe, then heel. **Q**

6. Left foot forward diag. to centre, partner in line. Heel. **S**

Note for Man

On the 1st step the Man should give a good body lead to his partner, and as he continues to spin, or turn, on the ball of his left foot (2nd step) he should bring his partner firmly to his right side, to enable her to complete her turn.

Man Rises at the end of the 1st step and lowers at the end of the 5th.

Man Sways to the right on the 2nd step (*not* the 3rd) and to the left on the 4th step.

LADY

Step No. *Count*

1. Left foot back turning body to right. Toe, then heel. **S**

2. **Close right heel to left heel, turning on left heel. Heel.** **Q**
3. **Continuing to turn to right on right foot, step to the side left foot, at same time allowing right foot to brush to left toe.** **Q**
4. **Replace right foot back and to side. Toe.** **Q**
5. **Back left foot, partner outside. Toe, then heel.** **Q**
6. **Back right foot. Toe, then heel.** **S**

General Notes

Technique is normal opposite of Man. Lady must feel the continuance of the turn from step 2 to step 3, and the brushing of the right foot towards left as the body continues to turn left.

Amalgamations

Although the length covered by most Foxtrot figures will determine their linking-up according to the room available, the fact that in many basic figures the last step of one figure becomes the 1st step of the next, means that the following facts should be noted.

When starting off, one must start with a Feather Step. This can lead to either a Reverse figure or into a Three-Step which in turn must preceded a Natural figure.

Here first is a simple group:

Feather Step, Reverse Turn, Change of Direction Step (to face diag. centre on next line of dance (for a small room).

Feather Step, Reverse Turn, Three-Step, Natural Turn.

Feather Step, Reverse Turn (first four steps) to Weave into Whisk.

Feather Step, Reverse Turn, Three-Step, Impetus Turn (at corner), Whisk, Reverse Turn, Three-Step, Natural Telemark.

In general, for down-the-room progression, Feather Steps, Three-Steps, Reverse Turns, and Weaves. At corners, Natural Turns, Natural Telemarks, Change of Direction Steps and Whisks.

Above all, those keen to become proficient at the Foxtrot must work hard at a smooth continuous gliding movement, making sure that one figure merges effortlessly into the next. Keep this in mind and develop the technical factors so essential to the Foxtrot: C.B.M., Sway, Rise and Fall.

Work at them, and they will give a satisfying reward!

[4]

THE TANGO

Introduction — Progressive Side Step — Reverse Turn — Progressive Link — Closed Promenade — Back Corté — Natural Promenade Turn — Four Step — Amalgamations

Introduction

It is a fact that whenever a Tango is played in a Ballroom or at any social function (which is usually a rarity!) most people make no attempt to get up and dance, but sit back and say 'Now, let's *watch* this dance!'

The result is that a handful of dancers on the floor are very keenly watched by all the rest! This sometimes has amusing results since there is *always* the type of person, who, realizing that he is being observed, will proceed to show off. Normally this kind of dancer, is not, to say the least of it, a very good one!

Yet the Tango is not in the least a hard dance.

In steps and construction it is actually a simple dance and has many factors which make it easier to dance than, say, the Foxtrot, or even some steps in the Waltz and Quickstep.

I suppose the real reason is that the Tango music is different to the more English-sounding dance rhythms and many people get the impression that the dance is slightly exotic and foreign.

The Tango is not hard, *it is simply a little different.*

The technique is different, because there is no Rise and Fall. All steps are taken on the heel when moving forward, and when moving back, the heel is lowered to the floor earlier than in the other dances.

The hold also is more compact, the Lady being held more to the Man's right hip than in the other dances (*see* Figs. 17 and 18). As a consequence, the Man's right arm is taken more round the Lady's back and the left forearm brought in at a sharper angle to 'balance up'.

The knees are kept more relaxed and the feet are picked up slightly off the floor and placed in a more deliberate fashion, in direct contrast to the other dances, in which we aim for a smooth, gliding action.

The steps themselves are taken more sharply.

Fig. 17.
The Man's Hold

Fig. 18.
The Lady's Hold

Man

Notice the altogether more intense hold. The knees are more relaxed, arms held lower. The right arm is taken further around Lady and she is held more on right hip. Both the right hip and shoulder are brought forward more. Note that the Lady's left hand is brought further round her partner and placed slightly under the arm. The Man's left foot and the Lady's right foot are in advance of their respective other foot.

Lady

Observe the lowered elbows, with the right hip and shoulder forward. Note that the Man's hand is held slightly lower and see how he holds his partner's wrist to give a clearer and sharper action. The Man's hand and arm is taken further round Lady.

Compare with Figs 7 and 8 and you will notice the more intense hold here.. As there is no Rise and Fall in the Tango, the Man must command more control over his partner by a firmer and more masterful hold. The knees are more flexed and the Lady is held more on the Man's right hip. Owing to the absence of Rise and Fall and the more compact hold, the weight and stance may appear more backward than in other dances, but this should not be very marked as the forward urge of the body caused by the weight being felt over the ball of the feet is still necessary.

To use a musical phrase — in a *staccato* fashion.

Also as a result of the Lady being held to the Man's right side with his right hand placed further around her, the Man finds that he has a tendency to 'lead' with his right shoulder so that when he takes a step forward with his left foot it moves *across* the body in a slightly sideways manner.

This results in the forward steps tending to curve towards the left.

Thus it will be seen that although the following descriptions will be found quite easy to follow, all the above characteristics of the Tango hold and walk must be noted, if one wants to catch the authentic sharpness of Tango figures.

Although many misconceptions are still held about it (a relic of the 'Roaring Twenties') the Tango today is as English as the Foxtrot and just as streamlined!

Although in Exhibition Dancing many Dips, Rolls and Sways are used to produce dramatic effects on the Ballroom floor, the basic figures of the Tango are quite easy to master, and when danced in a sharp or clipped fashion, are immensely enjoyable if the music is right.

Tango music is written in 2/4 time; that is, two beats in the bar, so that a slow step counts for one beat and a quick step half a beat. The modern 'sharp' Tango is best danced to what is known as the 'Milonga' rhythm, typified by such tunes as *La Cumparsita* or *Olé Guapa.* The old type of Tango rhythm, known as the 'Habanera' and typified by such tunes as *Jealousy* or *La Paloma,* is not now used.

Try the Tango; it's fun! And you will always have plenty of room to dance!

Progressive Side Step

The Progressive Side Step is the basic progressive movement of the Tango. It acts as a link between most other figures and can be danced any time the left foot is free.

Remember that every step forward with the left foot is taken with a left shoulder lead. This results in the left leg and foot being taken across the body, and the right foot moving slightly to the right, as well as forward.

As the description of the footwork will show, this often results in the side steps taken with the right foot being placed on the inside ledge of the right foot, and then going immediately on to the flat foot.

If a series of Progressive Side Steps are danced (and this is a good practice tip to get the feel of

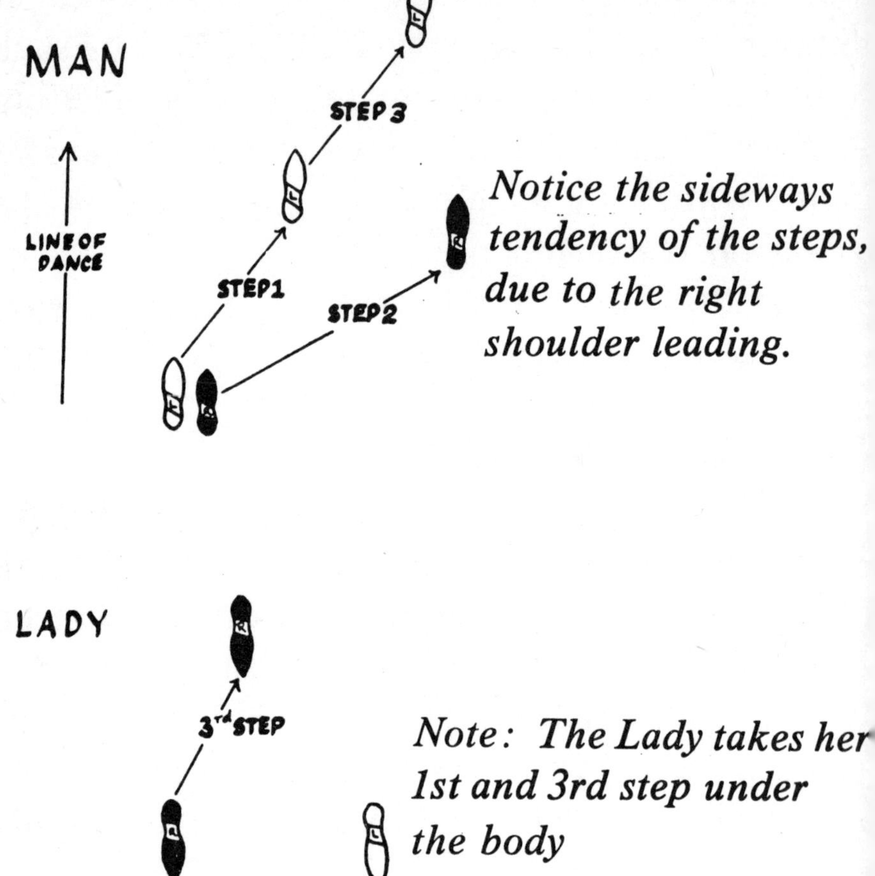

Fig. 19. The Progressive Side Step

the Tango whilst dancing a simple movement), it will be found that you will tend to move towards the left.

MAN

Step No.	*Count*
1. Left foot forward. Heel, flat.	**Q**
2. Right foot to side (and slightly back in relation to other foot). Inside edge of foot, flat.	**Q**
3. Left foot forward. Heel, flat.	**S**

LADY

Step No.	*Count*
1. Right foot back. Ball, the heel.	**Q**
2. Left foot to side (and slightly forward in relation to other foot). Inside edge of ball, heel, then flat.	**Q**
3. Right foot back. Ball.	**S**

General Notes

Remember that there is no Rise and Fall and no Sway, and that the left foot is taken across the body in C.B.M.P. All Reverse movements should be preceded by a Progressive Side Step. When dancing a right-hand figure it is preceded by a Progressive Link.

Reverse Turn

The Reverse Turn is a simple left-hand figure, the first three steps of which resemble the Open Turn of the Foxtrot.

Commence the figure any time the left foot is free and facing diag. centre. Finish facing the wall diag. Notice that unlike the turns in the other dances, the Reverse Turn is commenced with a quick, not a slow, step, the rhythm being QQS, QQS.

Note the descriptions referring to the edge of the foot.

MAN

Step No.		*Count*
1.	**Left foot forward diag. to centre, turning body to left. Heel, then flat.**	**Q**
2.	**Right foot to side across line of dance, still turning to left. Ball, then heel.**	**Q**
3.	**Left foot back down line of dance with left shoulder leading. Inside edge of ball, heel, then flat.**	**S**
4.	**Right foot back diag. to centre, turning body to left. Ball, then heel.**	**Q**
5.	**Left foot to side and slightly forward, still turning body to left to end facing diag. to wall. Inside edge of foot, then flat.**	**Q**

6. **Close right foot to left foot (slightly back—right toe level with left instep). Whole foot.** **S**

LADY

Step No. *Count*

1. **Right foot back diag. to centre, turning body to left. Ball, then heel.** **Q**
2. **Left foot closes loosely to right foot, still turning body to left. Now facing line of dance. Whole foot.** **Q**
3. **Right foot forward down line of dance with right shoulder leading. Heel, then flat.** **S**
4. **Left foot forward diag. to centre, turning body to left. Heel, then flat.** **Q**
5. **Right foot to side and slightly back, still turning body to left. Now backing diag. to wall. Inside edge of ball, heel, then flat.** **Q**
6. **Close left foot to right foot (slightly forward—left instep level with right toe). Whole foot.** **S**

General Notes

This turn can be followed by a Progressive Link into a Closed Promenade.

Progressive Link

Some of the most popular and characteristic figures in the Tango are the figures commencing in Promenade Position, that is a figure danced with Lady and Man opened out fan-wise.

The Progressive Link, therefore, is the preparatory movement which takes a couple from an 'in line' position to a Promenade Position.

The steps used are the first two steps of the Progressive Side Step, but as the Man takes his 2nd step to the side and slightly back, he turns his partner sharply to Promenade Position. Firm use of the base of the right hand is needed to turn the Lady to Promenade Position, but it is to be noted that the Man himself does not alter his body line by turning out as well. In point of fact he has a tendency to turn his body slightly to the right and by doing so helps to open out his partner.

MAN

Step No.		*Count*
1.	**Left foot forward diag. to wall. Heel, then flat.**	**Q**
2.	**Right foot to side, a small step (side and slightly back in relation to left foot). Now in Promenade Position. Inside edge of foot then flat, then inside edge of ball of left foot.**	**Q**

Continue by stepping to side on left foot in P.P.

LADY

Step No. *Count*

1. **Right foot back diag. to wall. Ball, then heel.** **Q**
2. **Left foot to side, a small step (side and slightly back in relation to right foot), turning body to right to end in Promenade Position. Now facing diag. to centre. Inside edge of ball, then heel, then flat, then inside edge of ball of right foot.** **Q**

Continue by stepping to the side right foot in P.P. into any Promenade figure.

Closed Promenade

The Closed Promenade is always preceded by the Progressive Link which finishes in Promenade Position, ready to move along the line of dance.

It is important to note that as the Man places 3rd step to the side (L.F.) he turns his partner square to him.

In this way the 4th—and closing-step—becomes a quiet movement.

Thus any step following will be commenced with the left foot diag. to wall, in line with partner. As the Lady is turned to P.P. she should turn her head sharply back to its original position. This is well worth the practice necessary to produce that Tango atmosphere. Avoid the temptation, in both Lady and Man, to look down when dancing a Promenade movement. It spoils the picture.

MAN

Step No.	*Count*
1. Left foot to side in Promenade Position along line of dance. Body facing diag. to wall. Heel, then flat.	**S**
2. Right foot forward and across in Promenade Position. (Take care not to open left side of body as this step is taken). Heel, then flat.	**Q**
3. Left foot to side and slightly forward. Inside edge of foot then flat.	**Q**
4. Close right foot to left foot (slightly back—right toe level with left instep). Whole foot.	**S**

LADY

Step No.	*Count*
1. Right foot to side in Promenade Position along line of dance. Body facing diag. to centre. Heel, then flat.	**S**

2. Left foot forward and across in Promenade Position. Heel, then flat. **Q**

3. Right foot to side and slightly back, having turned square to partner. Now backing diag. to wall. Inside edge of ball to heel, then flat. **Q**

4. Close left foot to right foot (slightly forward—left instep level with right toe). Whole foot. **S**

General Notes

When dancing the 2nd step, the Man must bring his leg well across the body and not allow the Lady to open out too wide.

The Lady should always try to keep her left hip back behind her partner's hip. The movement should not be danced hip-to-hip, as the angle created is too wide.

Back Corté

The Back Corté is a useful figure in that it allows a couple to move from a backward to a forward position. It can be danced any time a couple are backing the line of dance or diag. to centre, and the Man's left foot is free to move backward.

The Back Corté, however, is seldom danced as a separate figure, but is usually incorporated into other figures or as an ending as in the Natural Promenade Turn (*see* page 170).

MAN

Step No.	*Count*
1. Left foot back down line of dance, left shoulder leading. Inside edge of ball, then heel, then flat.	**S**
2. Right foot back diag. to centre, turning body to left. Ball, then heel.	**Q**
3. Left foot to side and slightly forward, still turning body to left. Now facing diag. to wall. Inside edge of foot, then flat.	**Q**
4. Close right foot to left foot (slightly back—right toe level with left instep). Whole foot.	**S**

LADY

Step No.	*Count*
1. Right foot forward, down line of dance, with right shoulder leading. Heel, then flat.	**S**
2. Left foot forward diag. to centre, turning body to left. Heel, then flat.	**Q**
3. Right foot to side still turning body to left. Now backing diag. to wall. Inside edge of ball, then heel, then flat.	**Q**

4. Close left foot to right foot (slightly forward—left instep level with right toe). Whole foot. **S**

General Notes

Follow this figure by stepping forward left foot diag. to wall into a walk or another Progressive Link, or a Progressive Side Step.

Natural Promenade Turn, with Rock and Back Corté

The Natural Promenade Turn has been aptly called the Spin Turn of the Tango. Best used at a corner, it also introduces the movement which typifies the Tango—the Rock.

The last four steps are actually the steps of the Corté, the last step of the Rock becoming the 1st step of the Corté.

Note that after step 3 is placed in position (L.F.) a Pivot is made on that foot in the manner of the Spin Turn of the Waltz or Quickstep. The right foot is held in front as the left foot pivots and is then extended slightly as the body continues to turn to the right. The 4th step then becomes the 1st step of the Rock.

The Lady, however, does not pivot with the Man. She steps to the side and back as he pivots, to get square to him.

Firm indication and pressure with the right hand by the Man is needed to turn the Lady, and at the same time turn square to her.

This is a delightful step and a very useful one. Try it.

MAN

Step No.		*Count*
1.	**Left foot to side in Promenade Position along line of dance. Body facing diag. to wall. Heel, then flat.**	**S**
2.	**Right foot forward in Promenade Position, commencing to turn body to right. Heel, then flat.**	**Q**
3.	**Left foot to side and slightly back, turning body to right. Now backing line of dance. Ball, then heel, then ball.**	**Q**
4.	**Right foot forward diag. to wall of new line of dance, turning body to right. Heel, then flat.**	**S**
5.	**Left foot to side and slightly back, still turning body to right. Now facing wall. Inside edge of ball, then heel.**	*The Rock* **Q**
6.	**Transfer weight forward to right foot —now backing diag. to centre. Inside edge of ball, then heel.**	**Q**

7.	**Left foot back, a small step with left shoulder leading. Inside edge of ball, then heel.**	**S**
8.	**Right foot back, to centre, turning body to left. Ball, then heel.**	**Q**
9.	**Left foot to side and slightly forward, still turning body to left. Now facing diag. to wall. Inside edge of foot, then flat.**	**Q**
10.	**Close right foot to left foot (slightly back—right toe level with instep). Whole foot.**	**S**

LADY

Step No.		*Count*
1.	**Right foot to side in Promenade Position along line of dance, body facing diag. to centre.**	**S**
2.	**Left foot forward and across in Promenade Position. Heel, then flat.**	**Q**
3.	**Right foot forward down line of dance and between partner's feet, turning body to right. Now facing line of dance. Heel, then flat.**	**Q**
4.	**Left foot to side and slightly back, turning body to right. Now backing diag. to wall of new line of dance. Ball, then heel.**	**S**

5. Transfer weight forward to right foot moving it slightly to right, still turning to right. Now backing wall. Heel, then flat. Q

6. Transfer weight back on to left foot, moving it slightly to left, a very small step. Now facing diag. to centre. Inside edge of ball, then heel. Q

7. Right foot forward, a very small step, diag. to centre. Heel, then flat. S

8. Left foot forward to centre, turning body to left. Heel, then flat. Q

9. Right foot to side and slightly back, still turning body to left. Now backing diag. to wall. Inside edge of ball, then heel, then flat. Q

10. Close left foot to right foot (slightly forward—left instep level with right toe). Whole foot. S

General Notes

The Man must use strong C.B.M. on steps 3 and 4 to help his pivoting action and to continue turning into the Rock.

It will help to master the Rock if the figure is practised separately by the Man, since he must learn to guide his partner into the Rocking action.

Try this:

	Count
Take a small step forward on to the right foot.	S
Rock back on to the left foot.	Q
Extend right very slightly forward and rock on to it.	Q
Extend left back and towards left.	S

Keep the feet and body quite flat; the body only rocks forward and back, not up and down!

Four Step

Apart from being a simple and enjoyable figure, the Four Step provides another way of turning the Lady into Promenade Position.

It can be danced when the left foot is free and the Man facing to wall. The Man's 2nd step must be a very small one to the side since he brings the Lady back *outside* him on step 3. As the Lady dances her last step, the Man should exert pressure at the base of his right hand to turn the Lady to P.P.

The Lady should remember to turn her head sharply to the right as she turns to P.P.

MAN

Step No.		*Count*
1.	**Left foot forward to wall slightly across the body. Heel, flat.**	**Q**
2.	**Right foot to side and slightly back, facing diag. to wall. Ball, then heel.**	**Q**
3.	**Left foot back, moving diag. to centre against line of dance, partner outside. Ball, then heel.**	**Q**
4.	**Close right foot to left foot (slightly back—right toe level with left instep), turn partner to Promenade Position. Ball, then heel.**	**Q**

LADY

Step No.		*Count*
1.	**Right foot back to wall slightly across the body. Ball, then heel.**	**Q**
2.	**Left foot to side and slightly forward, pointing diag. to centre against the line of dance. Whole foot.**	**Q**
3.	**Right foot forward, outside partner. Heel, and then flat.**	**Q**
4.	**Close left foot to right foot (slightly back —left toe level with right instep), turning to right on ball of right foot to end in Promenade Position, facing diag. to centre. Ball, then heel.**	**Q**

The above figure can be followed by any Promenade figure.

Amalgamations

Learning to dance the Tango becomes really worth while, once the simple steps have been mastered, if only for the exciting rhythm and the many interesting tunes that are used.

The dance also has the advantage that it does not need so much room as, say, the Foxtrot, and can easily be adapted to a very small space.

The compact and intense hold should not be exaggerated, but the deliberate placing of the feet, at the same time picking them up slightly off the floor as a step is taken, should always be felt, and is an essential part of the expression of the Tango.

A simple amalgamation to start with is as follows:

Start with two walking steps, curving them towards the centre of the room, then dance a Reverse Turn. This will finish you facing wall diag.

Then dance two more walks curving towards the line of dance and a Progressive Side step, curving to centre and then into another Reverse Turn.

This will keep you continuously moving and getting the feel of both steps and rhythm. It can be repeated *ad lib.*

Once having got the feel of the dance, try the following:

Two walks, Reverse Turn, as before, then into the Four Step and a Closed Promenade. This also can be repeated, and if finished at a corner, a Corté can be used to face your next line of dance.

Now try this amalgamation, starting at one end of the room:

Two walks to centre, Reverse Turn, Progressive Link to Closed Promenade, then the Four Step to Natural Promenade Turn, into the corner and finish along the next line of dance.

By combining all three above amalgamations, one can have an interesting routine all round the room. As soon as you feel you have mastered this, the various groups of figures can be varied, since in almost every case one figure will lead into another.

Always remember: if at a loss to know what figure to use, you can always use the walking steps until you feel that you are in a position to dance a step that you feel sure of.

One last thing, like all the other dances, practise this rewarding dance as much as possible.

To the Man I would say: learn the Tango, for it is an extremely useful accomplishment. And to the Lady: a good Lady Tango dancer is always in demand!

[5]

SOCIAL RHYTHM DANCING

Introduction — Quarter Turn to right — Quarter Turn to left — Natural Pivot Turn — Back Corté — Side Step — Promenade Step

Introduction

Although modern Ballroom dancing has reached a high peak of perfection, particularly in this country, its devotees at competition level are comparatively few. To most of us, dancing is a pleasant relaxation and provides a common meeting ground on social occasions, as well as being an excellent medium for making friends.

At the same time, there are many people who, whatever they take up, wish to do it well.

A serious study of the previous chapters will certainly help the enthusiast learn to dance properly. It is at this stage that dancing ceases to be mere entertainment and becomes an achievement. There are then endless opportunities in the many Dance Studios throughout the country to become extremely proficient through the medium of Medal Tests, which are held in the Bronze, Silver, Gold and Award medal grades.

It also cannot be denied that there are many occasions when even elementary Ballroom dancing is rendered very difficult, if not almost impossible, by the conditions that prevail: usually too many people in too confined a space!

Dinner dances, night clubs, parties in the home, etc., seldom provide enough space for even a compact form of Quickstep, to say nothing of the Foxtrot. In fact, any couple attempting to dance normal length steps would soon cause havoc!

Yet, the band or pianist (or the record player!) *will* start up and people *will* want to dance, particularly as dancing is the finest social ice-breaker in the world!

The answer to the problem is *rhythm dancing.*

Rhythm, or Social, dancing can be extremely satisfying and has the additional advantage that it can be danced to *any* 4/4 dance tune and at any speed.

Even more useful is the fact that the steps can be as small as you care to make them, since the rhythm is expressed more in the body and in the flexing movement of the knees, than in the length of stride.

This is done by alternately flexing and straightening the knees as a step is taken.

Try a few walking steps to a slow count of music each time and try to feel the rhythmic 'lilt' as follows:

Commence feet together, knees relaxed.

Take a small step forward with right foot, at the same time straightening the left, or supporting, knee.

As the weight of the body is taken on to the right foot, keep the right leg momentarily straight and then relax it.

Then bring your left foot forward, at the same time straightening the right knee.

You will then find that each step with each foot produces a slight up and down movement in the legs (but not the body!), a sort of 'lilting' movement obtained through the legs and knees.

Practise the count of four slows, dance four walking steps, at the same time saying 'straight-relax, straight-relax, straight-relax'.

Having felt this slight up and down movement, then apply it to all the steps, whether forward or back, to the side or closing.

The effect of a rhythmic Walk can be heightened if, when dancing slow or leading steps, artificial simulation of C.B.M. is used. In other words, as one leg moves forward turn the opposite hip and shoulder towards it. Remember that the body should move only forward and back, *not* up and down. The up and down effect is created through the relaxing and straightening of the knees.

This rhythmic walking can be great fun and one can really express any Foxtrot or Quickstep rhythm through it, whatever the speed being played.

At first, it will be found much easier to dance to the slowest possible tempo, to get the flexing knee action needed.

The steps themselves are actually modified Quickstep figures, as you will discover, so there is not a lot to learn in that respect. Concentrate therefore on the rhythmic interpretation which characterizes Social Rhythm dancing!

The steps used are as follows:

Quarter Turn to right — *Reverse Pivot Turn*
Quarter Turn to left — *Back Corté*
Natural Pivot Turn — *Side Step*
Promenade Step (*Conversation Piece*)

Since the steps taken are so small and the Lady's steps are the normal opposite to Man's, only the Man's steps are given.

Quarter Turn to Right

Commence facing diag. to wall.

Step No.	*Count*
1. Forward left foot.	**S**
2. Forward right foot turning right.	**S**
3. Left foot to side, still turning right.	**Q**
4. Close right foot to left foot, now backing diag. centre.	**Q**

Quarter Turn to Left

Step No.	*Count*
1. Back left foot diag. to centre.	**S**
2. Back right foot turning left.	**S**
3. Very small step side and slightly forward left foot, still turning left.	**Q**
4. Close right to left foot, finish facing diag. to wall.	**Q**

Natural Pivot Turn

Throughout this movement the body continues to turn to the right, and on steps 1 and 2 a slight pivoting action is felt. This can be obtained by allowing the body to keep turning with the slight use of C.B.M.

Step No.	*Count*
1. Small step back left foot, turning body left.	**S**
2. Transfer weight to right foot, still turning body, and pivot on flat of right foot.	**S**
3. Left foot to side, still turning right.	**Q**
4. Close right foot to left foot.	**Q**

Note: This figure can be used at a corner, turning about three-quarters of a turn to the right. It is not advisable to attempt it along the room.

Reverse Pivot Turn

As in the Natural Pivot Turn, on steps 1 and 2 obtain a slight pivoting action to the left. It will be noted that where the Natural Pivot was commenced backward, the Reverse Pivot Turn is commenced forward, and providing the steps are kept very small this figure can be danced along the room. If this is attempted, then two complete Reverse Pivot Turns should be danced, making half a turn on each one.

Step No.	*Count*
1. Left foot forward turning left.	**S**
2. Very small step back right foot still turning left.	**S**

3. Small step side left foot, still turning. **Q**
4. Close right foot towards left foot. **Q**

Note: The pivoting action will be found easier if the second step is not moved at all but is slightly released from the floor and the weight replaced. Try to think of the Reverse Pivot Turn as a turning movement created entirely by the body, with the weight simply being transferred from one foot to the other in time with the music.

Back Corté

This is a useful figure as it enables a couple to keep with the flow of the other dancers and yet move backward (invaluable if the floor is so crowded that you do not even have *room* to turn!)

It is also useful to dance at a corner, and by turning to the left throughout you will face the next line of dance.

Step No.	*Count*
1. Back left down line of dance, left shoulder leading.	**S**
2. Back right foot.	**S**
3. Small step to side left foot.	**Q**
4. Close right foot towards left foot.	**Q**

Repeat the above figure as necessary to travel down the room.

The Side Step

The Side Step is another figure that can keep you flowing with the rest of the dancers by repeating the complete movement several times moving sideways, down the room.

Step No.	*Count*
1. Left foot to side (facing wall).	**S**
2. Close right foot towards left foot.	**S**
3. Side left foot.	**Q**
4. Close right foot towards left foot.	**Q**

Note: A very rhythmic and interesting effect can be achieved in this figure if a slight sway from the hips to the right is made as the 2nd step is taken to the side, straightening as the feet close.

The Promenade Step

This is probably one of the most popular figures in rhythm dancing since it enables a couple to dance side-by-side in Promenade Position and indulge in the light-hearted conversation usually so pleasant a part of all social functions.

Commence by dancing two walks (left foot, right foot) and turning your partner to Promenade Position on step 2. The following left foot is then taken in Promenade Position as below.

Step No.	*Count*
1. Left foot sideways and forward down the line of dance, in P.P.	**S**
2. Cross right foot over left and forward in P.P.	**S**
3. Left foot to the side and slightly in P.P.	**Q**
4. Close right foot to left foot in P.P.	**Q**

Note: This movement can be repeated several times, still staying in Promenade Position, and the normal dance hold can be resumed by closing your partner square on the last two quick steps (side and close) of the Promenade Side Step. (The Man's cue for this is obviously when the conversation dries up!)

Remember if you want to dance with the minimum of effort and floor space, keep the steps as small as possible and feel the rhythm in the legs and knees. Do not bounce up and down and do not make your steps jerky. I am sure that you will then thoroughly enjoy Social Rhythm dancing!